# TEACHER'S PET PUBLICATIONS

## PUZZLE PACK
## for
## Where the Red Fern Grows

based on the book by
Wilson Rawls

Written by
William T. Collins

© 2006 Teacher's Pet Publications
All Rights Reserved

The materials in this packet are copyrighted
by Teacher's Pet Publications, Inc.

These pages may be duplicated by the purchaser
for use in the purchaser's own classroom.

Copying any of these materials and distributing them
for any other purpose is a violation of the copyright laws.

© 2005 Teacher's Pet Publications, Inc.
www.tpet.com

## INTRODUCTION
If you already own the LitPlan for this title, this Puzzle Pack will refresh your Unit Resource Materials and Vocabulary Resource Materials sections plus give you additional materials you can substitute into the tests. If you do not already have a complete LitPlan, these pages will give you some supplemental materials to use with your own plan. There are two main groups of materials: one set for unit words (such as characters' names, symbols, places, etc.) and one set for vocabulary words associated with the book.

## WORD LIST
There is a word list for both the unit words and the vocabulary words. These lists show you which words are being used in the materials and the clues or definitions being used for those words. You may want to give students a word list with clues/definitions to help them, or you may want students to only have a word list (without clues/definitions) if you want them to work a little harder. Both are available for duplication. The word lists can also be your "calling key" for the bingo games.

## FILL IN THE BLANK AND MATCHING
There are 4 each of the fill in the blank and matching worksheets for both the unit and vocabulary words. These pages can be used either as extra worksheets for students or as objective parts of a unit test. They can be done individually if students need extra help or as a whole class activity to review the material covered.

## MAGIC SQUARES
The magic squares not only reinforce the material covered but also work on reasoning and math skills. Many teachers have told us that their students really enjoy doing these!

## WORD SEARCH PUZZLES
The word search words go in all directions, as indicated on your answer keys. Two of the word search puzzles have the clues listed rather than the words. This makes the puzzle a little more difficult, but it reinforces the material better. Two word search puzzles have words only for students who find the clue puzzles too difficult.

## CROSSWORD PUZZLES
Both unit and vocabulary word sections have 4 crossword puzzles.

## BINGO CARDS
There are 32 individual bingo cards for the unit words and 32 individual bingo cards for the vocabulary words. You can use your word list as a "call list," calling the words at random and marking them off of your list as you go, or you could use the flash cards by cutting them apart and drawing the words at random from a hat (or box or whatever). To make a better review, you might ask for the definition and spelling of each word as you call it out—or you could call out the definitions and have students tell you the words they need to look for on the puzzle.

## JUGGLE LETTERS
The vocabulary juggle letter game is intended to help students learn the spellings of the words. One sheet has the definitions listed on it as an extra help for students who need it or to reinforce the definitions if you choose to do so.

## FLASH CARDS
We've included a set of vocabulary flash cards you can duplicate, cut, and fold for your students. Some teachers make a few sets for general use by the class; others make a set for each student. Some teachers duplicate them for each student and have the students cut & fold their own. You can cut out just the words and put them in a hat, have each student pick out one word and write the definition and a sentence for that word. Students then swap words and papers, with the next student adding a sentence of his own under the last one. You can have students swap as many times as you like. Each time the student will read the sentences written prior to his own and then add a sentence. You can cut out the words and definitions separately and play "I Have; Who Has?" Each student in the room draws a word and definition. The first student says, "I have (the name of the word). Who has the definition?" The student with the definition reads it then says, "I have (the name of the vocabulary word she has). Who has the definition?" The round continues until all words and definitions have been given.

**Where The Red Fern Grows Word List**

| No. | Word | Clue/Definition |
|---|---|---|
| 1. | ANN | Smart but gun-shy: Little ___ |
| 2. | BAKING | Billy used a K.C.___Powder can for a bank |
| 3. | BET | Grandpa made one with the Pritchard boys |
| 4. | BILLY | Was afflicted with puppy love |
| 5. | BLUE | The Pritchard's hound: Old ___ |
| 6. | BOBCAT | Billy thought the hounds had treed one |
| 7. | BOTTOMS | Location of the big sycamore tree |
| 8. | CAP | Mama made one from Billy's first coon skin |
| 9. | CHEROKEE | Mama's Indian heritage |
| 10. | COATS | Fad for coon skin ones raised the price of skins |
| 11. | CONTEST | Grandpa entered the hounds in one |
| 12. | COON | Billy didn't want to kill it: ghost ___ |
| 13. | DAN | Strong and aggressive: Old ___ |
| 14. | DEPOT | Where Billy picked up his puppies |
| 15. | ENGLAND | Where coonskin coat fad was: New ___ |
| 16. | FERN | Grew on a sacred spot: red ___ |
| 17. | FIFTY | Dollar amount Billy saved |
| 18. | FLOWERS | Billy put them on Rubin's grave |
| 19. | FORTY | Dollar cost of the hounds |
| 20. | GOD | Thought about and talked to frequently by Billy |
| 21. | GOLD | Cup Billy gave to his youngest sister |
| 22. | GRANDPA | Sent away for the dogs |
| 23. | GUN | Billy's other desire |
| 24. | ILLINOIS | River near the bottoms |
| 25. | JUDGE | Was amazed at Billy's dogs |
| 26. | KENTUCKY | Location of kennel |
| 27. | LION | Attacked Billy and the dogs: mountain ___ |
| 28. | MAMA | Prayed for a way to move to town |
| 29. | MARSHAL | Rescued Billy from the fight with the town children |
| 30. | OKLAHOMA | State where Billy lived |
| 31. | OZARKS | Mountain setting of novel |
| 32. | PAPA | Gave Billy three steel traps |
| 33. | POST | Where the ghost coon hid: gate ___ |
| 34. | PRITCHARD | Rubin and Rainie's last name |
| 35. | RAINIE | Was excited on the hunt for the ghost coon |
| 36. | RAWLS | Author |
| 37. | REFLECTION | Billy saw his for the first time on his trip to town |
| 38. | RINGTAIL | Nickname for a raccoon: Mr. ___ |
| 39. | RUBIN | Fell on the axe and died |
| 40. | SACK | Billy carried the puppies home in one: gunny ___ |
| 41. | SAMIE | Curious cat |
| 42. | SILVER | Cup Little Ann won at the beauty contest |
| 43. | SLEET | Weather during last night of the coon hunting contest |
| 44. | STORE | Where Grandpa worked |
| 45. | TALEQUAH | Town Billy walked to for the dogs |
| 46. | TEN | Dollar amount Billy spent on gifts for the family |
| 47. | THREE | Number of Billy's sisters |
| 48. | TWO | Dollar amount of Grandpa's bet with the Pritchard boys |
| 49. | WHOOP | Sound Billy made to the hounds |

Where The Red Fern Grows Fill In The Blanks 1

_____

_____

_____

_____

_____

_____

_____

_____

_____

_____

_____

_____

_____

_____

_____

_____

_____

_____

_____

_____

1. State where Billy lived
2. Location of kennel
3. Was amazed at Billy's dogs
4. Billy put them on Rubin's grave
5. Weather during last night of the coon hunting contest
6. Attacked Billy and the dogs: mountain ___
7. Billy saw his for the first time on his trip to town
8. Cup Little Ann won at the beauty contest
9. Dollar cost of the hounds
10. Gave Billy three steel traps
11. The Pritchard's hound: Old ___
12. Strong and aggressive: Old ___
13. Where the ghost coon hid: gate ___
14. Grew on a sacred spot: red ___
15. Nickname for a raccoon: Mr. ___
16. Mama made one from Billy's first coon skin
17. Smart but gun-shy: Little ___
18. Where Grandpa worked
19. Billy used a K.C. ___ Powder can for a bank
20. Sound Billy made to the hounds

Where The Red Fern Grows Fill In The Blanks 1 Answer Key

| OKLAHOMA | 1. State where Billy lived |
| KENTUCKY | 2. Location of kennel |
| JUDGE | 3. Was amazed at Billy's dogs |
| FLOWERS | 4. Billy put them on Rubin's grave |
| SLEET | 5. Weather during last night of the coon hunting contest |
| LION | 6. Attacked Billy and the dogs: mountain ___ |
| REFLECTION | 7. Billy saw his for the first time on his trip to town |
| SILVER | 8. Cup Little Ann won at the beauty contest |
| FORTY | 9. Dollar cost of the hounds |
| PAPA | 10. Gave Billy three steel traps |
| BLUE | 11. The Pritchard's hound: Old ___ |
| DAN | 12. Strong and aggressive: Old ___ |
| POST | 13. Where the ghost coon hid: gate ___ |
| FERN | 14. Grew on a sacred spot: red ___ |
| RINGTAIL | 15. Nickname for a raccoon: Mr. ___ |
| CAP | 16. Mama made one from Billy's first coon skin |
| ANN | 17. Smart but gun-shy: Little ___ |
| STORE | 18. Where Grandpa worked |
| BAKING | 19. Billy used a K.C. ___ Powder can for a bank |
| WHOOP | 20. Sound Billy made to the hounds |

Where The Red Fern Grows Fill In The Blanks 2

_____

_____

_____

_____

_____

_____

_____

_____

_____

_____

_____

_____

_____

_____

_____

_____

_____

_____

_____

_____

1. Fad for coon skin ones raised the price of skins
2. Billy carried the puppies home in one: gunny ___
3. Mama made one from Billy's first coon skin
4. Dollar amount Billy spent on gifts for the family
5. Author
6. Rescued Billy from the fight with the town children
7. Billy used a K.C.___Powder can for a bank
8. Grandpa made one with the Pritchard boys
9. Town Billy walked to for the dogs
10. Grew on a sacred spot: red ___
11. Grandpa entered the hounds in one
12. Number of Billy's sisters
13. Billy put them on Rubin's grave
14. Billy didn't want to kill it: ghost ___
15. Cup Little Ann won at the beauty contest
16. Cup Billy gave to his youngest sister
17. Dollar amount Billy saved
18. Mountain setting of novel
19. Was excited on the hunt for the ghost coon
20. The Pritchard's hound: Old ___

Where The Red Fern Grows Fill In The Blanks 2 Answer Key

| Answer | # | Clue |
|---|---|---|
| COATS | 1. | Fad for coon skin ones raised the price of skins |
| SACK | 2. | Billy carried the puppies home in one: gunny ___ |
| CAP | 3. | Mama made one from Billy's first coon skin |
| TEN | 4. | Dollar amount Billy spent on gifts for the family |
| RAWLS | 5. | Author |
| MARSHAL | 6. | Rescued Billy from the fight with the town children |
| BAKING | 7. | Billy used a K.C. ___ Powder can for a bank |
| BET | 8. | Grandpa made one with the Pritchard boys |
| TALEQUAH | 9. | Town Billy walked to for the dogs |
| FERN | 10. | Grew on a sacred spot: red ___ |
| CONTEST | 11. | Grandpa entered the hounds in one |
| THREE | 12. | Number of Billy's sisters |
| FLOWERS | 13. | Billy put them on Rubin's grave |
| COON | 14. | Billy didn't want to kill it: ghost ___ |
| SILVER | 15. | Cup Little Ann won at the beauty contest |
| GOLD | 16. | Cup Billy gave to his youngest sister |
| FIFTY | 17. | Dollar amount Billy saved |
| OZARKS | 18. | Mountain setting of novel |
| RAINIE | 19. | Was excited on the hunt for the ghost coon |
| BLUE | 20. | The Pritchard's hound: Old ___ |

Where The Red Fern Grows Fill In The Blanks 3

_____  1. Where Billy picked up his puppies

_____  2. Rubin and Rainie's last name

_____  3. River near the bottoms

_____  4. Location of kennel

_____  5. Dollar amount Billy spent on gifts for the family

_____  6. Billy's other desire

_____  7. Number of Billy's sisters

_____  8. Weather during last night of the coon hunting contest

_____  9. The Pritchard's hound: Old ___

_____  10. Billy put them on Rubin's grave

_____  11. Thought about and talked to frequently by Billy

_____  12. State where Billy lived

_____  13. Was afflicted with puppy love

_____  14. Nickname for a raccoon: Mr. ___

_____  15. Attacked Billy and the dogs: mountain ___

_____  16. Was excited on the hunt for the ghost coon

_____  17. Dollar cost of the hounds

_____  18. Mama's Indian heritage

_____  19. Mama made one from Billy's first coon skin

_____  20. Dollar amount of Grandpa's bet with the Pritchard boys

Where The Red Fern Grows Fill In The Blanks 3 Answer Key

| | | |
|---|---|---|
| DEPOT | 1. | Where Billy picked up his puppies |
| PRITCHARD | 2. | Rubin and Rainie's last name |
| ILLINOIS | 3. | River near the bottoms |
| KENTUCKY | 4. | Location of kennel |
| TEN | 5. | Dollar amount Billy spent on gifts for the family |
| GUN | 6. | Billy's other desire |
| THREE | 7. | Number of Billy's sisters |
| SLEET | 8. | Weather during last night of the coon hunting contest |
| BLUE | 9. | The Pritchard's hound: Old ___ |
| FLOWERS | 10. | Billy put them on Rubin's grave |
| GOD | 11. | Thought about and talked to frequently by Billy |
| OKLAHOMA | 12. | State where Billy lived |
| BILLY | 13. | Was afflicted with puppy love |
| RINGTAIL | 14. | Nickname for a raccoon: Mr. ___ |
| LION | 15. | Attacked Billy and the dogs: mountain ___ |
| RAINIE | 16. | Was excited on the hunt for the ghost coon |
| FORTY | 17. | Dollar cost of the hounds |
| CHEROKEE | 18. | Mama's Indian heritage |
| CAP | 19. | Mama made one from Billy's first coon skin |
| TWO | 20. | Dollar amount of Grandpa's bet with the Pritchard boys |

Where The Red Fern Grows Fill In The Blanks 4

_____

_____

_____

_____

_____

_____

_____

_____

_____

_____

_____

_____

_____

_____

_____

_____

_____

_____

_____

_____

1. Where coonskin coat fad was: New ___
2. Grew on a sacred spot: red ___
3. Mountain setting of novel
4. The Pritchard's hound: Old ___
5. Billy carried the puppies home in one: gunny ___
6. Billy thought the hounds had treed one
7. Smart but gun-shy: Little ___
8. Author
9. Mama made one from Billy's first coon skin
10. Weather during last night of the coon hunting contest
11. Nickname for a raccoon: Mr. ___
12. Fell on the axe and died
13. Location of the big sycamore tree
14. Grandpa entered the hounds in one
15. Was excited on the hunt for the ghost coon
16. Was amazed at Billy's dogs
17. Cup Little Ann won at the beauty contest
18. Thought about and talked to frequently by Billy
19. Billy didn't want to kill it: ghost ___
20. Cup Billy gave to his youngest sister

Where The Red Fern Grows Fill In The Blanks 4 Answer Key

|  |  |  |
|---|---|---|
| ENGLAND | 1. | Where coonskin coat fad was: New ___ |
| FERN | 2. | Grew on a sacred spot: red ___ |
| OZARKS | 3. | Mountain setting of novel |
| BLUE | 4. | The Pritchard's hound: Old ___ |
| SACK | 5. | Billy carried the puppies home in one: gunny ___ |
| BOBCAT | 6. | Billy thought the hounds had treed one |
| ANN | 7. | Smart but gun-shy: Little ___ |
| RAWLS | 8. | Author |
| CAP | 9. | Mama made one from Billy's first coon skin |
| SLEET | 10. | Weather during last night of the coon hunting contest |
| RINGTAIL | 11. | Nickname for a raccoon: Mr. ___ |
| RUBIN | 12. | Fell on the axe and died |
| BOTTOMS | 13. | Location of the big sycamore tree |
| CONTEST | 14. | Grandpa entered the hounds in one |
| RAINIE | 15. | Was excited on the hunt for the ghost coon |
| JUDGE | 16. | Was amazed at Billy's dogs |
| SILVER | 17. | Cup Little Ann won at the beauty contest |
| GOD | 18. | Thought about and talked to frequently by Billy |
| COON | 19. | Billy didn't want to kill it: ghost ___ |
| GOLD | 20. | Cup Billy gave to his youngest sister |

Where The Red Fern Grows Matching 1

___ 1. SLEET  A. Number of Billy's sisters
___ 2. BET  B. Grew on a sacred spot: red ___
___ 3. KENTUCKY  C. Was amazed at Billy's dogs
___ 4. BOBCAT  D. Location of kennel
___ 5. FLOWERS  E. Billy thought the hounds had treed one
___ 6. PRITCHARD  F. Gave Billy three steel traps
___ 7. DEPOT  G. Dollar amount Billy spent on gifts for the family
___ 8. PAPA  H. Sound Billy made to the hounds
___ 9. MARSHAL  I. Rubin and Rainie's last name
___10. TEN  J. Billy saw his for the first time on his trip to town
___11. WHOOP  K. Grandpa made one with the Pritchard boys
___12. SACK  L. Where Billy picked up his puppies
___13. RUBIN  M. Dollar amount of Grandpa's bet with the Pritchard boys
___14. OKLAHOMA  N. Billy carried the puppies home in one: gunny ___
___15. GRANDPA  O. Fell on the axe and died
___16. TWO  P. Where the ghost coon hid: gate ___
___17. REFLECTION  Q. Grandpa entered the hounds in one
___18. CONTEST  R. Where coonskin coat fad was: New ___
___19. FERN  S. Sent away for the dogs
___20. POST  T. Cup Little Ann won at the beauty contest
___21. ENGLAND  U. Weather during last night of the coon hunting contest
___22. SILVER  V. State where Billy lived
___23. JUDGE  W. Fad for coon skin ones raised the price of skins
___24. COATS  X. Rescued Billy from the fight with the town children
___25. THREE  Y. Billy put them on Rubin's grave

Where The Red Fern Grows Matching 1 Answer Key

| | | | |
|---|---|---|---|
| U - 1. | SLEET | A. | Number of Billy's sisters |
| K - 2. | BET | B. | Grew on a sacred spot: red ___ |
| D - 3. | KENTUCKY | C. | Was amazed at Billy's dogs |
| E - 4. | BOBCAT | D. | Location of kennel |
| Y - 5. | FLOWERS | E. | Billy thought the hounds had treed one |
| I - 6. | PRITCHARD | F. | Gave Billy three steel traps |
| L - 7. | DEPOT | G. | Dollar amount Billy spent on gifts for the family |
| F - 8. | PAPA | H. | Sound Billy made to the hounds |
| X - 9. | MARSHAL | I. | Rubin and Rainie's last name |
| G -10. | TEN | J. | Billy saw his for the first time on his trip to town |
| H -11. | WHOOP | K. | Grandpa made one with the Pritchard boys |
| N -12. | SACK | L. | Where Billy picked up his puppies |
| O -13. | RUBIN | M. | Dollar amount of Grandpa's bet with the Pritchard boys |
| V -14. | OKLAHOMA | N. | Billy carried the puppies home in one: gunny ___ |
| S -15. | GRANDPA | O. | Fell on the axe and died |
| M -16. | TWO | P. | Where the ghost coon hid: gate ___ |
| J - 17. | REFLECTION | Q. | Grandpa entered the hounds in one |
| Q -18. | CONTEST | R. | Where coonskin coat fad was: New ___ |
| B -19. | FERN | S. | Sent away for the dogs |
| P -20. | POST | T. | Cup Little Ann won at the beauty contest |
| R -21. | ENGLAND | U. | Weather during last night of the coon hunting contest |
| T -22. | SILVER | V. | State where Billy lived |
| C -23. | JUDGE | W. | Fad for coon skin ones raised the price of skins |
| W -24. | COATS | X. | Rescued Billy from the fight with the town children |
| A -25. | THREE | Y. | Billy put them on Rubin's grave |

Where The Red Fern Grows Matching 2

___ 1. STORE　　　　　　A. Sent away for the dogs
___ 2. DAN　　　　　　　B. Billy didn't want to kill it: ghost ___
___ 3. GUN　　　　　　　C. Dollar cost of the hounds
___ 4. ENGLAND　　　　 D. Location of kennel
___ 5. SACK　　　　　　 E. Attacked Billy and the dogs: mountain ___
___ 6. DEPOT　　　　　　F. Billy carried the puppies home in one: gunny ___
___ 7. BAKING　　　　　 G. Where Grandpa worked
___ 8. REFLECTION　　　 H. Billy put them on Rubin's grave
___ 9. KENTUCKY　　　　 I. Location of the big sycamore tree
___10. GOD　　　　　　　J. Rescued Billy from the fight with the town children
___11. SAMIE　　　　　　K. Grandpa entered the hounds in one
___12. FORTY　　　　　　L. Cup Billy gave to his youngest sister
___13. RUBIN　　　　　　M. Where the ghost coon hid: gate ___
___14. PAPA　　　　　　 N. Curious cat
___15. ILLINOIS　　　　 O. Billy's other desire
___16. GOLD　　　　　　 P. River near the bottoms
___17. BOTTOMS　　　　　Q. Thought about and talked to frequently by Billy
___18. FLOWERS　　　　　R. Gave Billy three steel traps
___19. GRANDPA　　　　　S. Billy saw his for the first time on his trip to town
___20. BET　　　　　　　T. Billy used a K.C.___Powder can for a bank
___21. LION　　　　　　 U. Grandpa made one with the Pritchard boys
___22. POST　　　　　　 V. Fell on the axe and died
___23. CONTEST　　　　　W. Where Billy picked up his puppies
___24. MARSHAL　　　　　X. Strong and aggressive: Old ___
___25. COON　　　　　　 Y. Where coonskin coat fad was: New ___

Where The Red Fern Grows Matching 2 Answer Key

| | | |
|---|---|---|
| G - 1. STORE | A. | Sent away for the dogs |
| X - 2. DAN | B. | Billy didn't want to kill it: ghost ___ |
| O - 3. GUN | C. | Dollar cost of the hounds |
| Y - 4. ENGLAND | D. | Location of kennel |
| F - 5. SACK | E. | Attacked Billy and the dogs: mountain ___ |
| W - 6. DEPOT | F. | Billy carried the puppies home in one: gunny ___ |
| T - 7. BAKING | G. | Where Grandpa worked |
| S - 8. REFLECTION | H. | Billy put them on Rubin's grave |
| D - 9. KENTUCKY | I. | Location of the big sycamore tree |
| Q -10. GOD | J. | Rescued Billy from the fight with the town children |
| N -11. SAMIE | K. | Grandpa entered the hounds in one |
| C -12. FORTY | L. | Cup Billy gave to his youngest sister |
| V -13. RUBIN | M. | Where the ghost coon hid: gate ___ |
| R -14. PAPA | N. | Curious cat |
| P -15. ILLINOIS | O. | Billy's other desire |
| L -16. GOLD | P. | River near the bottoms |
| I -17. BOTTOMS | Q. | Thought about and talked to frequently by Billy |
| H -18. FLOWERS | R. | Gave Billy three steel traps |
| A -19. GRANDPA | S. | Billy saw his for the first time on his trip to town |
| U -20. BET | T. | Billy used a K.C.___Powder can for a bank |
| E -21. LION | U. | Grandpa made one with the Pritchard boys |
| M -22. POST | V. | Fell on the axe and died |
| K -23. CONTEST | W. | Where Billy picked up his puppies |
| J -24. MARSHAL | X. | Strong and aggressive: Old ___ |
| B -25. COON | Y. | Where coonskin coat fad was: New ___ |

Where The Red Fern Grows Matching 3

___ 1. COON  A. State where Billy lived
___ 2. KENTUCKY  B. Fell on the axe and died
___ 3. CAP  C. Dollar amount of Grandpa's bet with the Pritchard boys
___ 4. TWO  D. Location of kennel
___ 5. FIFTY  E. Weather during last night of the coon hunting contest
___ 6. SAMIE  F. Dollar amount Billy spent on gifts for the family
___ 7. THREE  G. Where Billy picked up his puppies
___ 8. RUBIN  H. Prayed for a way to move to town
___ 9. SACK  I. Fad for coon skin ones raised the price of skins
___ 10. GUN  J. Sent away for the dogs
___ 11. COATS  K. Cup Billy gave to his youngest sister
___ 12. SLEET  L. Rescued Billy from the fight with the town children
___ 13. RAINIE  M. The Pritchard's hound: Old ___
___ 14. TEN  N. Mama made one from Billy's first coon skin
___ 15. MAMA  O. Sound Billy made to the hounds
___ 16. OKLAHOMA  P. Cup Little Ann won at the beauty contest
___ 17. SILVER  Q. Curious cat
___ 18. WHOOP  R. Billy didn't want to kill it: ghost ___
___ 19. DEPOT  S. Rubin and Rainie's last name
___ 20. MARSHAL  T. Billy carried the puppies home in one: gunny ___
___ 21. CONTEST  U. Grandpa entered the hounds in one
___ 22. GOLD  V. Billy's other desire
___ 23. GRANDPA  W. Was excited on the hunt for the ghost coon
___ 24. PRITCHARD  X. Number of Billy's sisters
___ 25. BLUE  Y. Dollar amount Billy saved

Where The Red Fern Grows Matching 3 Answer Key

| | | | |
|---|---|---|---|
| R - 1. | COON | A. | State where Billy lived |
| D - 2. | KENTUCKY | B. | Fell on the axe and died |
| N - 3. | CAP | C. | Dollar amount of Grandpa's bet with the Pritchard boys |
| C - 4. | TWO | D. | Location of kennel |
| Y - 5. | FIFTY | E. | Weather during last night of the coon hunting contest |
| Q - 6. | SAMIE | F. | Dollar amount Billy spent on gifts for the family |
| X - 7. | THREE | G. | Where Billy picked up his puppies |
| B - 8. | RUBIN | H. | Prayed for a way to move to town |
| T - 9. | SACK | I. | Fad for coon skin ones raised the price of skins |
| V -10. | GUN | J. | Sent away for the dogs |
| I - 11. | COATS | K. | Cup Billy gave to his youngest sister |
| E -12. | SLEET | L. | Rescued Billy from the fight with the town children |
| W -13. | RAINIE | M. | The Pritchard's hound: Old ___ |
| F -14. | TEN | N. | Mama made one from Billy's first coon skin |
| H -15. | MAMA | O. | Sound Billy made to the hounds |
| A -16. | OKLAHOMA | P. | Cup Little Ann won at the beauty contest |
| P -17. | SILVER | Q. | Curious cat |
| O -18. | WHOOP | R. | Billy didn't want to kill it: ghost ___ |
| G -19. | DEPOT | S. | Rubin and Rainie's last name |
| L -20. | MARSHAL | T. | Billy carried the puppies home in one: gunny ___ |
| U -21. | CONTEST | U. | Grandpa entered the hounds in one |
| K -22. | GOLD | V. | Billy's other desire |
| J -23. | GRANDPA | W. | Was excited on the hunt for the ghost coon |
| S -24. | PRITCHARD | X. | Number of Billy's sisters |
| M -25. | BLUE | Y. | Dollar amount Billy saved |

Where The Red Fern Grows Matching 4

___ 1. BOTTOMS          A. Rubin and Rainie's last name
___ 2. ILLINOIS         B. Curious cat
___ 3. PRITCHARD        C. Mama made one from Billy's first coon skin
___ 4. ANN              D. Grandpa entered the hounds in one
___ 5. BET              E. Weather during last night of the coon hunting contest
___ 6. TALEQUAH         F. Fell on the axe and died
___ 7. POST             G. Strong and aggressive: Old ___
___ 8. OKLAHOMA         H. Billy didn't want to kill it: ghost ___
___ 9. COON             I. Gave Billy three steel traps
___10. RUBIN            J. Sent away for the dogs
___11. DAN              K. Fad for coon skin ones raised the price of skins
___12. CAP              L. Smart but gun-shy: Little ___
___13. PAPA             M. The Pritchard's hound: Old ___
___14. REFLECTION       N. Thought about and talked to frequently by Billy
___15. GOD              O. Town Billy walked to for the dogs
___16. SLEET            P. Location of the big sycamore tree
___17. BLUE             Q. Author
___18. RAWLS            R. River near the bottoms
___19. COATS            S. Where coonskin coat fad was: New ___
___20. GRANDPA          T. State where Billy lived
___21. ENGLAND          U. Where the ghost coon hid: gate ___
___22. TWO              V. Grandpa made one with the Pritchard boys
___23. SAMIE            W. Billy saw his for the first time on his trip to town
___24. STORE            X. Dollar amount of Grandpa's bet with the Pritchard boys
___25. CONTEST          Y. Where Grandpa worked

Where The Red Fern Grows Matching 4 Answer Key

| | | |
|---|---|---|
| P - 1. | BOTTOMS | A. Rubin and Rainie's last name |
| R - 2. | ILLINOIS | B. Curious cat |
| A - 3. | PRITCHARD | C. Mama made one from Billy's first coon skin |
| L - 4. | ANN | D. Grandpa entered the hounds in one |
| V - 5. | BET | E. Weather during last night of the coon hunting contest |
| O - 6. | TALEQUAH | F. Fell on the axe and died |
| U - 7. | POST | G. Strong and aggressive: Old ___ |
| T - 8. | OKLAHOMA | H. Billy didn't want to kill it: ghost ___ |
| H - 9. | COON | I. Gave Billy three steel traps |
| F - 10. | RUBIN | J. Sent away for the dogs |
| G - 11. | DAN | K. Fad for coon skin ones raised the price of skins |
| C - 12. | CAP | L. Smart but gun-shy: Little ___ |
| I - 13. | PAPA | M. The Pritchard's hound: Old ___ |
| W - 14. | REFLECTION | N. Thought about and talked to frequently by Billy |
| N - 15. | GOD | O. Town Billy walked to for the dogs |
| E - 16. | SLEET | P. Location of the big sycamore tree |
| M - 17. | BLUE | Q. Author |
| Q - 18. | RAWLS | R. River near the bottoms |
| K - 19. | COATS | S. Where coonskin coat fad was: New ___ |
| J - 20. | GRANDPA | T. State where Billy lived |
| S - 21. | ENGLAND | U. Where the ghost coon hid: gate ___ |
| X - 22. | TWO | V. Grandpa made one with the Pritchard boys |
| B - 23. | SAMIE | W. Billy saw his for the first time on his trip to town |
| Y - 24. | STORE | X. Dollar amount of Grandpa's bet with the Pritchard boys |
| D - 25. | CONTEST | Y. Where Grandpa worked |

Where The Red Fern Grows Magic Squares 1

Match the definition with the vocabulary word. Put your answers in the magic squares below. When your answers are correct, all columns and rows will add to the same number.

A. TALEQUAH        G. ANN            M. CAP
B. RINGTAIL        H. TEN            N. SACK
C. CHEROKEE        I. BAKING         O. MAMA
D. RAINIE          J. TWO            P. DAN
E. COON            K. PRITCHARD
F. THREE           L. SAMIE

1. Nickname for a raccoon: Mr. ___
2. Smart but gun-shy: Little ___
3. Rubin and Rainie's last name
4. Billy carried the puppies home in one: gunny ___
5. Mama made one from Billy's first coon skin
6. Curious cat
7. Dollar amount Billy spent on gifts for the family
8. Town Billy walked to for the dogs
9. Strong and aggressive: Old ___
10. Billy used a K.C.___Powder can for a bank
11. Billy didn't want to kill it: ghost ___
12. Was excited on the hunt for the ghost coon
13. Mama's Indian heritage
14. Number of Billy's sisters
15. Dollar amount of Grandpa's bet with the Pritchard boys
16. Prayed for a way to move to town

| A= | B= | C= | D= |
|---|---|---|---|
| E= | F= | G= | H= |
| I= | J= | K= | L= |
| M= | N= | O= | P= |

Where The Red Fern Grows Magic Squares 1 Answer Key

Match the definition with the vocabulary word. Put your answers in the magic squares below. When your answers are correct, all columns and rows will add to the same number.

A. TALEQUAH
B. RINGTAIL
C. CHEROKEE
D. RAINIE
E. COON
F. THREE
G. ANN
H. TEN
I. BAKING
J. TWO
K. PRITCHARD
L. SAMIE
M. CAP
N. SACK
O. MAMA
P. DAN

1. Nickname for a raccoon: Mr. __
2. Smart but gun-shy: Little ___
3. Rubin and Rainie's last name
4. Billy carried the puppies home in one: gunny ___
5. Mama made one from Billy's first coon skin
6. Curious cat
7. Dollar amount Billy spent on gifts for the family
8. Town Billy walked to for the dogs
9. Strong and aggressive: Old ___
10. Billy used a K.C.___Powder can for a bank
11. Billy didn't want to kill it: ghost ___
12. Was excited on the hunt for the ghost coon
13. Mama's Indian heritage
14. Number of Billy's sisters
15. Dollar amount of Grandpa's bet with the Pritchard boys
16. Prayed for a way to move to town

| A=8 | B=1 | C=13 | D=12 |
|---|---|---|---|
| E=11 | F=14 | G=2 | H=7 |
| I=10 | J=15 | K=3 | L=6 |
| M=5 | N=4 | O=16 | P=9 |

Where The Red Fern Grows Magic Squares 2

Match the definition with the vocabulary word. Put your answers in the magic squares below. When your answers are correct, all columns and rows will add to the same number.

A. CONTEST
B. FLOWERS
C. GUN
D. FIFTY
E. FERN
F. TEN
G. BET
H. ILLINOIS
I. TWO
J. PRITCHARD
K. BOTTOMS
L. RUBIN
M. CHEROKEE
N. GOD
O. BLUE
P. MAMA

1. Grandpa entered the hounds in one
2. Thought about and talked to frequently by Billy
3. Rubin and Rainie's last name
4. Grew on a sacred spot: red ___
5. Grandpa made one with the Pritchard boys
6. Fell on the axe and died
7. Prayed for a way to move to town
8. Billy's other desire
9. The Pritchard's hound: Old ___
10. Dollar amount Billy saved
11. River near the bottoms
12. Location of the big sycamore tree
13. Dollar amount of Grandpa's bet with the Pritchard boys
14. Dollar amount Billy spent on gifts for the family
15. Billy put them on Rubin's grave
16. Mama's Indian heritage

| A= | B= | C= | D= |
|---|---|---|---|
| E= | F= | G= | H= |
| I= | J= | K= | L= |
| M= | N= | O= | P= |

Where The Red Fern Grows Magic Squares 2 Answer Key

Match the definition with the vocabulary word. Put your answers in the magic squares below. When your answers are correct, all columns and rows will add to the same number.

A. CONTEST
B. FLOWERS
C. GUN
D. FIFTY
E. FERN
F. TEN
G. BET
H. ILLINOIS
I. TWO
J. PRITCHARD
K. BOTTOMS
L. RUBIN
M. CHEROKEE
N. GOD
O. BLUE
P. MAMA

1. Grandpa entered the hounds in one
2. Thought about and talked to frequently by Billy
3. Rubin and Rainie's last name
4. Grew on a sacred spot: red ___
5. Grandpa made one with the Pritchard boys
6. Fell on the axe and died
7. Prayed for a way to move to town
8. Billy's other desire
9. The Pritchard's hound: Old ___
10. Dollar amount Billy saved
11. River near the bottoms
12. Location of the big sycamore tree
13. Dollar amount of Grandpa's bet with the Pritchard boys
14. Dollar amount Billy spent on gifts for the family
15. Billy put them on Rubin's grave
16. Mama's Indian heritage

| A=1 | B=15 | C=8 | D=10 |
|---|---|---|---|
| E=4 | F=14 | G=5 | H=11 |
| I=13 | J=3 | K=12 | L=6 |
| M=16 | N=2 | O=9 | P=7 |

Where The Red Fern Grows Magic Squares 3

Match the definition with the vocabulary word. Put your answers in the magic squares below. When your answers are correct, all columns and rows will add to the same number.

A. RUBIN
B. GOLD
C. FLOWERS
D. SILVER
E. BLUE
F. THREE
G. MARSHAL
H. SLEET
I. DEPOT
J. RAINIE
K. ENGLAND
L. POST
M. BOBCAT
N. BET
O. MAMA
P. PAPA

1. Billy put them on Rubin's grave
2. Was excited on the hunt for the ghost coon
3. Number of Billy's sisters
4. Prayed for a way to move to town
5. Gave Billy three steel traps
6. The Pritchard's hound: Old ___
7. Where Billy picked up his puppies
8. Cup Little Ann won at the beauty contest
9. Billy thought the hounds had treed one
10. Weather during last night of the coon hunting contest
11. Where the ghost coon hid: gate ___
12. Fell on the axe and died
13. Cup Billy gave to his youngest sister
14. Where coonskin coat fad was: New ___
15. Rescued Billy from the fight with the town children
16. Grandpa made one with the Pritchard boys

| A= | B= | C= | D= |
| --- | --- | --- | --- |
| E= | F= | G= | H= |
| I= | J= | K= | L= |
| M= | N= | O= | P= |

Where The Red Fern Grows Magic Squares 3 Answer Key

Match the definition with the vocabulary word. Put your answers in the magic squares below. When your answers are correct, all columns and rows will add to the same number.

A. RUBIN
B. GOLD
C. FLOWERS
D. SILVER
E. BLUE
F. THREE
G. MARSHAL
H. SLEET
I. DEPOT
J. RAINIE
K. ENGLAND
L. POST
M. BOBCAT
N. BET
O. MAMA
P. PAPA

1. Billy put them on Rubin's grave
2. Was excited on the hunt for the ghost coon
3. Number of Billy's sisters
4. Prayed for a way to move to town
5. Gave Billy three steel traps
6. The Pritchard's hound: Old ___
7. Where Billy picked up his puppies
8. Cup Little Ann won at the beauty contest
9. Billy thought the hounds had treed one
10. Weather during last night of the coon hunting contest
11. Where the ghost coon hid: gate ___
12. Fell on the axe and died
13. Cup Billy gave to his youngest sister
14. Where coonskin coat fad was: New ___
15. Rescued Billy from the fight with the town children
16. Grandpa made one with the Pritchard boys

| A=12 | B=13 | C=1  | D=8  |
|------|------|------|------|
| E=6  | F=3  | G=15 | H=10 |
| I=7  | J=2  | K=14 | L=11 |
| M=9  | N=16 | O=4  | P=5  |

Where The Red Fern Grows Magic Squares 4

Match the definition with the vocabulary word. Put your answers in the magic squares below. When your answers are correct, all columns and rows will add to the same number.

A. BOBCAT
B. GUN
C. TWO
D. GRANDPA
E. OZARKS
F. OKLAHOMA
G. FERN
H. JUDGE
I. RAINIE
J. BET
K. SILVER
L. GOD
M. MARSHAL
N. BLUE
O. DAN
P. MAMA

1. Was amazed at Billy's dogs
2. Billy thought the hounds had treed one
3. Billy's other desire
4. Grew on a sacred spot: red ___
5. Grandpa made one with the Pritchard boys
6. Strong and aggressive: Old ___
7. Prayed for a way to move to town
8. Was excited on the hunt for the ghost coon
9. Cup Little Ann won at the beauty contest
10. The Pritchard's hound: Old ___
11. Rescued Billy from the fight with the town children
12. Thought about and talked to frequently by Billy
13. Mountain setting of novel
14. Sent away for the dogs
15. Dollar amount of Grandpa's bet with the Pritchard boys
16. State where Billy lived

| A= | B= | C= | D= |
|---|---|---|---|
| E= | F= | G= | H= |
| I= | J= | K= | L= |
| M= | N= | O= | P= |

Where The Red Fern Grows Magic Squares 4 Answer Key

Match the definition with the vocabulary word. Put your answers in the magic squares below. When your answers are correct, all columns and rows will add to the same number.

A. BOBCAT
B. GUN
C. TWO
D. GRANDPA
E. OZARKS
F. OKLAHOMA
G. FERN
H. JUDGE
I. RAINIE
J. BET
K. SILVER
L. GOD
M. MARSHAL
N. BLUE
O. DAN
P. MAMA

1. Was amazed at Billy's dogs
2. Billy thought the hounds had treed one
3. Billy's other desire
4. Grew on a sacred spot: red ___
5. Grandpa made one with the Pritchard boys
6. Strong and aggressive: Old ___
7. Prayed for a way to move to town
8. Was excited on the hunt for the ghost coon
9. Cup Little Ann won at the beauty contest
10. The Pritchard's hound: Old ___
11. Rescued Billy from the fight with the town children
12. Thought about and talked to frequently by Billy
13. Mountain setting of novel
14. Sent away for the dogs
15. Dollar amount of Grandpa's bet with the Pritchard boys
16. State where Billy lived

| A=2 | B=3 | C=15 | D=14 |
|---|---|---|---|
| E=13 | F=16 | G=4 | H=1 |
| I=8 | J=5 | K=9 | L=12 |
| M=11 | N=10 | O=6 | P=7 |

Where The Red Fern Grows Word Search 1

Words are placed backwards, forward, diagonally, up and down. Clues listed below can help you find the words. Circle the hidden vocabulary words in the maze.

| | | | | | | | | | | | | | | | | | |
|---|---|---|---|---|---|---|---|---|---|---|---|---|---|---|---|---|---|
| B | J | U | D | G | E | D | A | N | M | A | R | S | H | A | L | T | F |
| T | O | F | F | O | O | N | P | W | B | I | K | A | P | K | I | W | L |
| N | M | T | D | L | F | D | O | S | N | N | M | A | I | R | O | O | B |
| B | A | A | T | D | O | Y | S | G | P | J | P | P | T | N | N | H | R |
| A | M | L | Y | O | X | W | T | S | I | L | V | E | R | T | I | K | T |
| K | A | E | Z | M | M | A | E | W | V | N | F | C | B | S | M | E | J |
| I | J | Q | R | M | I | S | N | R | K | P | I | Q | G | E | P | E | X |
| N | C | U | S | L | H | J | O | T | S | V | F | C | X | T | S | R | F |
| G | S | A | C | K | X | J | I | S | P | P | T | G | O | N | P | H | N |
| Z | H | H | R | K | E | N | T | U | C | K | Y | Y | C | O | A | T | S |
| K | R | B | S | J | G | C | C | Z | H | T | L | S | O | C | N | G | Q |
| G | A | N | Y | T | P | H | E | S | R | L | L | H | E | Y | S | R | K |
| B | W | I | Y | E | P | Z | L | O | I | B | W | R | V | P | A | A | T |
| V | L | B | Z | N | R | E | F | B | Z | J | O | J | R | J | M | N | M |
| C | S | U | L | V | Q | H | E | B | G | T | Q | B | A | C | I | D | L |
| L | A | R | E | C | Y | S | R | E | S | P | B | R | C | N | E | P | L |
| D | E | P | O | T | P | R | I | T | C | H | A | R | D | A | N | A | Z |
| G | U | N | E | N | G | L | A | N | D | S | L | E | E | T | T | Y | B |

Attacked Billy and the dogs: mountain ___ (4)
Author (5)
Billy carried the puppies home in one: gunny ___ (4)
Billy didn't want to kill it: ghost ___ (4)
Billy put them on Rubin's grave (7)
Billy saw his for the first time on his trip to town (10)
Billy thought the hounds had treed one (6)
Billy used a K.C.___Powder can for a bank (6)
Billy's other desire (3)
Cup Billy gave to his youngest sister (4)
Cup Little Ann won at the beauty contest (6)
Curious cat (5)
Dollar amount Billy saved (5)
Dollar amount Billy spent on gifts for the family (3)
Dollar amount of Grandpa's bet with the Pritchard boys (3)
Dollar cost of the hounds (5)
Fad for coon skin ones raised the price of skins (5)
Fell on the axe and died (5)
Gave Billy three steel traps (4)
Grandpa entered the hounds in one (7)
Grandpa made one with the Pritchard boys (3)
Grew on a sacred spot: red ___ (4)
Location of kennel (8)
Location of the big sycamore tree (7)
Mama made one from Billy's first coon skin (3)
Nickname for a raccoon: Mr. __ (8)
Number of Billy's sisters (5)
Prayed for a way to move to town (4)
Rescued Billy from the fight with the town children (7)
Rubin and Rainie's last name (9)
Sent away for the dogs (7)
Smart but gun-shy: Little ___ (3)
Sound Billy made to the hounds (5)
Strong and aggressive: Old ___ (3)
The Pritchard's hound: Old ___ (4)
Thought about and talked to frequently by Billy (3)
Town Billy walked to for the dogs (8)
Was afflicted with puppy love (5)
Was amazed at Billy's dogs (5)
Was excited on the hunt for the ghost coon (6)
Weather during last night of the coon hunting contest (5)
Where Billy picked up his puppies (5)
Where Grandpa worked (5)
Where coonskin coat fad was: New ___ (7)
Where the ghost coon hid: gate ___ (4)

Where The Red Fern Grows Word Search 1 Answer Key

Words are placed backwards, forward, diagonally, up and down. Clues listed below can help you find the words. Circle the hidden vocabulary words in the maze.

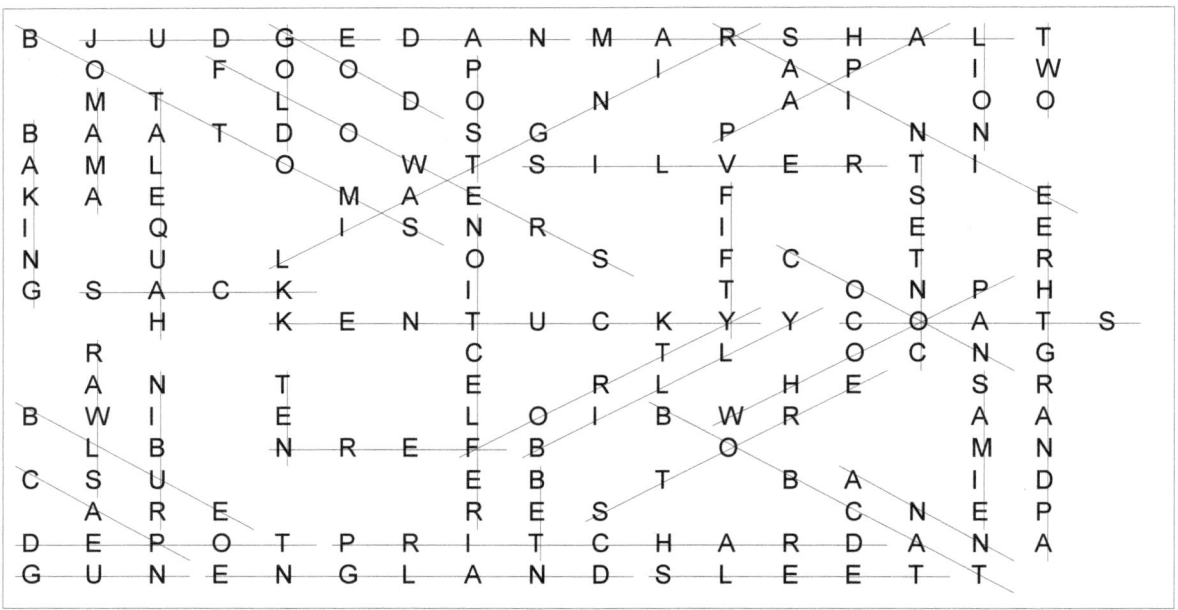

Attacked Billy and the dogs: mountain ___ (4)
Author (5)
Billy carried the puppies home in one: gunny ___ (4)
Billy didn't want to kill it: ghost ___ (4)
Billy put them on Rubin's grave (7)
Billy saw his for the first time on his trip to town (10)
Billy thought the hounds had treed one (6)
Billy used a K.C.___Powder can for a bank (6)
Billy's other desire (3)
Cup Billy gave to his youngest sister (4)
Cup Little Ann won at the beauty contest (6)
Curious cat (5)
Dollar amount Billy saved (5)
Dollar amount Billy spent on gifts for the family (3)
Dollar amount of Grandpa's bet with the Pritchard boys (3)
Dollar cost of the hounds (5)
Fad for coon skin ones raised the price of skins (5)
Fell on the axe and died (5)
Gave Billy three steel traps (4)
Grandpa entered the hounds in one (7)
Grandpa made one with the Pritchard boys (3)
Grew on a sacred spot: red ___ (4)

Location of kennel (8)
Location of the big sycamore tree (7)
Mama made one from Billy's first coon skin (3)
Nickname for a raccoon: Mr. ___ (8)
Number of Billy's sisters (5)
Prayed for a way to move to town (4)
Rescued Billy from the fight with the town children (7)
Rubin and Rainie's last name (9)
Sent away for the dogs (7)
Smart but gun-shy: Little ___ (3)
Sound Billy made to the hounds (5)
Strong and aggressive: Old ___ (3)
The Pritchard's hound: Old ___ (4)
Thought about and talked to frequently by Billy (3)
Town Billy walked to for the dogs (8)
Was afflicted with puppy love (5)
Was amazed at Billy's dogs (5)
Was excited on the hunt for the ghost coon (6)
Weather during last night of the coon hunting contest (5)
Where Billy picked up his puppies (5)
Where Grandpa worked (5)
Where coonskin coat fad was: New ___ (7)
Where the ghost coon hid: gate ___ (4)

Where The Red Fern Grows Word Search 2

Words are placed backwards, forward, diagonally, up and down. Clues listed below can help you find the words. Circle the hidden vocabulary words in the maze.

```
C H E R O K E E I M A S B I L L Y F
G F Y K C U T N E K M T I O Z L K D
R L J V L P Y D V O T A F L B X V C
A O Q B W O G H T R L O M I V C H V
N W C N J S B T T U H C N J F E A V
D E W O L T O E C B S J P X J T R T
P R W G N B D R F I L P U R P H Y K
A S M N T T T O B N E Z A D B R D T
V X B D W C E T B E E Y H P G E A F
K M O Z A R K S G K T Y H S A E N R
T A L E Q U A H T A T H V Q I E R L
M M P Q H C M R J R N D G N T D I W
X A T X K W H O O P R N I W D E N S
C G R V C S T F R X I A O L N P G F
V C K S T L T D T K R L O D M O T G
J C O P H W Q F A D Z G N T Z T A B
G U N O F A Z B S I O N I L L I I D
L I O N N R L F E R N E G O D X L M
```

Attacked Billy and the dogs: mountain ___ (4)
Author (5)
Billy carried the puppies home in one: gunny ___ (4)
Billy didn't want to kill it: ghost ___ (4)
Billy put them on Rubin's grave (7)
Billy thought the hounds had treed one (6)
Billy used a K.C. ___ Powder can for a bank (6)
Billy's other desire (3)
Cup Billy gave to his youngest sister (4)
Cup Little Ann won at the beauty contest (6)
Curious cat (5)
Dollar amount Billy saved (5)
Dollar amount Billy spent on gifts for the family (3)
Dollar amount of Grandpa's bet with the Pritchard boys (3)
Dollar cost of the hounds (5)
Fad for coon skin ones raised the price of skins (5)
Fell on the axe and died (5)
Gave Billy three steel traps (4)
Grandpa entered the hounds in one (7)
Grandpa made one with the Pritchard boys (3)
Grew on a sacred spot: red ___ (4)
Location of kennel (8)
Location of the big sycamore tree (7)

Mama made one from Billy's first coon skin (3)
Mama's Indian heritage (8)
Mountain setting of novel (6)
Nickname for a raccoon: Mr ___ (8)
Number of Billy's sisters (5)
Prayed for a way to move to town (4)
Rescued Billy from the fight with the town children (7)
River near the bottoms (8)
Sent away for the dogs (7)
Smart but gun-shy: Little ___ (3)
Sound Billy made to the hounds (5)
Strong and aggressive: Old ___ (3)
The Pritchard's hound: Old ___ (4)
Thought about and talked to frequently by Billy (3)
Town Billy walked to for the dogs (8)
Was afflicted with puppy love (5)
Was amazed at Billy's dogs (5)
Was excited on the hunt for the ghost coon (6)
Weather during last night of the coon hunting contest (5)
Where Billy picked up his puppies (5)
Where Grandpa worked (5)
Where coonskin coat fad was: New ___ (7)
Where the ghost coon hid: gate ___ (4)

Where The Red Fern Grows Word Search 2 Answer Key

Words are placed backwards, forward, diagonally, up and down. Clues listed below can help you find the words. Circle the hidden vocabulary words in the maze.

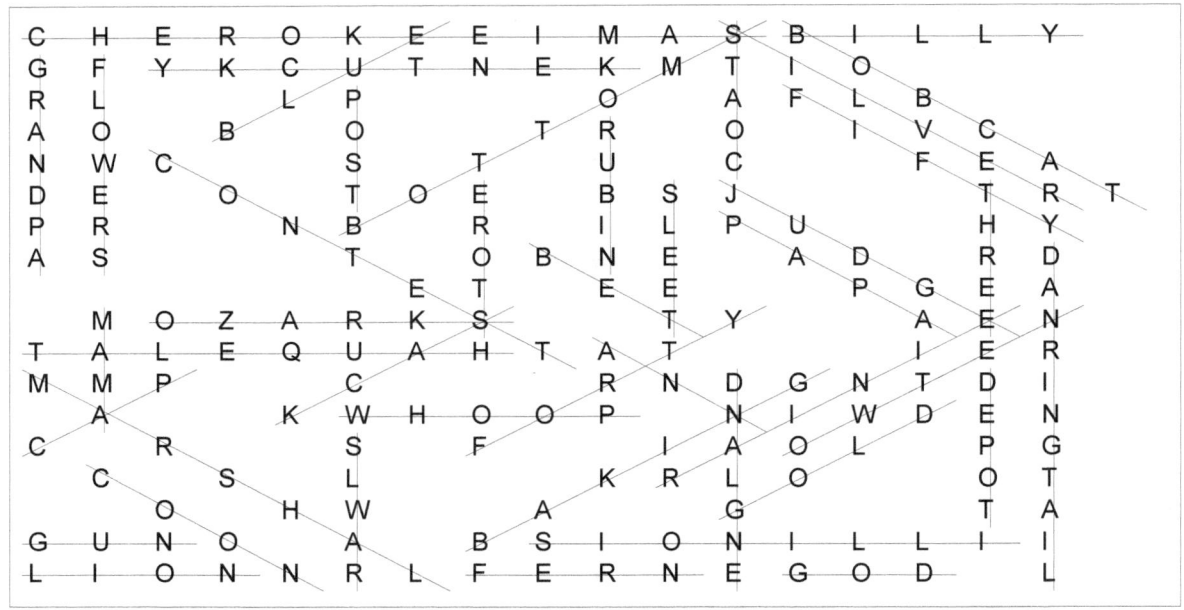

Attacked Billy and the dogs: mountain ___ (4)
Author (5)
Billy carried the puppies home in one: gunny ___ (4)
Billy didn't want to kill it: ghost ___ (4)
Billy put them on Rubin's grave (7)
Billy thought the hounds had treed one (6)
Billy used a K.C. ___ Powder can for a bank (6)
Billy's other desire (3)
Cup Billy gave to his youngest sister (4)
Cup Little Ann won at the beauty contest (6)
Curious cat (5)
Dollar amount Billy saved (5)
Dollar amount Billy spent on gifts for the family (3)
Dollar amount of Grandpa's bet with the Pritchard boys (3)
Dollar cost of the hounds (5)
Fad for coon skin ones raised the price of skins (5)
Fell on the axe and died (5)
Gave Billy three steel traps (4)
Grandpa entered the hounds in one (7)
Grandpa made one with the Pritchard boys (3)
Grew on a sacred spot: red ___ (4)
Location of kennel (8)
Location of the big sycamore tree (7)

Mama made one from Billy's first coon skin (3)
Mama's Indian heritage (8)
Mountain setting of novel (6)
Nickname for a raccoon: Mr. ___ (8)
Number of Billy's sisters (5)
Prayed for a way to move to town (4)
Rescued Billy from the fight with the town children (7)
River near the bottoms (8)
Sent away for the dogs (7)
Smart but gun-shy: Little ___ (3)
Sound Billy made to the hounds (5)
Strong and aggressive: Old ___ (3)
The Pritchard's hound: Old ___ (4)
Thought about and talked to frequently by Billy (3)
Town Billy walked to for the dogs (8)
Was afflicted with puppy love (5)
Was amazed at Billy's dogs (5)
Was excited on the hunt for the ghost coon (6)
Weather during last night of the coon hunting contest (5)
Where Billy picked up his puppies (5)
Where Grandpa worked (5)
Where coonskin coat fad was: New ___ (7)
Where the ghost coon hid: gate ___ (4)

Where The Red Fern Grows Word Search 3

Words are placed backwards, forward, diagonally, up and down. Words listed below are included in the maze. Circle the hidden vocabulary words in the maze.

| W | N | C | B | Z | K | O | D | J | S | B | O | T | T | O | M | S | M |
|---|---|---|---|---|---|---|---|---|---|---|---|---|---|---|---|---|---|
| M | H | F | L | L | J | H | K | E | I | A | O | T | J | W | C | Z | N |
| G | O | O | C | V | U | W | L | L | P | H | M | B | F | U | B | M | Y |
| V | Z | R | O | R | M | E | L | B | A | O | L | I | C | K | D | K | T |
| W | A | T | A | P | A | Y | B | A | R | H | T | X | E | A | C | G | X |
| Z | R | Y | T | R | R | L | Q | K | S | G | O | V | F | U | T | B | E |
| Y | K | E | S | X | S | T | F | I | F | T | Y | M | T | P | R | D | W |
| M | S | M | N | F | H | N | C | N | V | C | F | N | A | E | R | W | Y |
| M | A | F | V | G | A | N | L | G | R | M | E | C | V | A | C | N | T |
| L | C | M | C | R | L | S | A | C | K | K | Y | L | H | J | U | R | C |
| F | A | Q | A | W | A | A | J | X | S | J | I | C | G | G | D | G | R |
| S | P | M | P | V | P | I | N | J | T | S | T | Z | L | V | C | U | F |
| Q | D | K | C | A | M | N | N | D | O | I | D | Q | I | C | B | D | X |
| X | N | X | V | R | P | N | R | I | R | T | Q | A | O | I | O | Q | Q |
| T | A | L | E | Q | U | A | H | P | E | F | E | R | N | D | L | O | G |
| M | R | T | W | D | W | D | B | B | T | H | R | E | E | K | R | O | N |
| T | G | I | L | L | I | N | O | I | S | F | T | L | M | P | W | B | Q |
| G | O | D | S | R | E | W | O | L | F | S | L | E | E | T | S | O | P |

| ANN | COON | GOLD | OKLAHOMA | SAMIE |
| BAKING | DAN | GRANDPA | OZARKS | SILVER |
| BET | DEPOT | GUN | PAPA | SLEET |
| BILLY | ENGLAND | ILLINOIS | POST | STORE |
| BLUE | FERN | JUDGE | PRITCHARD | TALEQUAH |
| BOBCAT | FIFTY | KENTUCKY | RAINIE | TEN |
| BOTTOMS | FLOWERS | LION | RAWLS | THREE |
| CAP | FORTY | MAMA | RUBIN | TWO |
| COATS | GOD | MARSHAL | SACK | WHOOP |

Where The Red Fern Grows Word Search 3 Answer Key

Words are placed backwards, forward, diagonally, up and down. Words listed below are included in the maze. Circle the hidden vocabulary words in the maze.

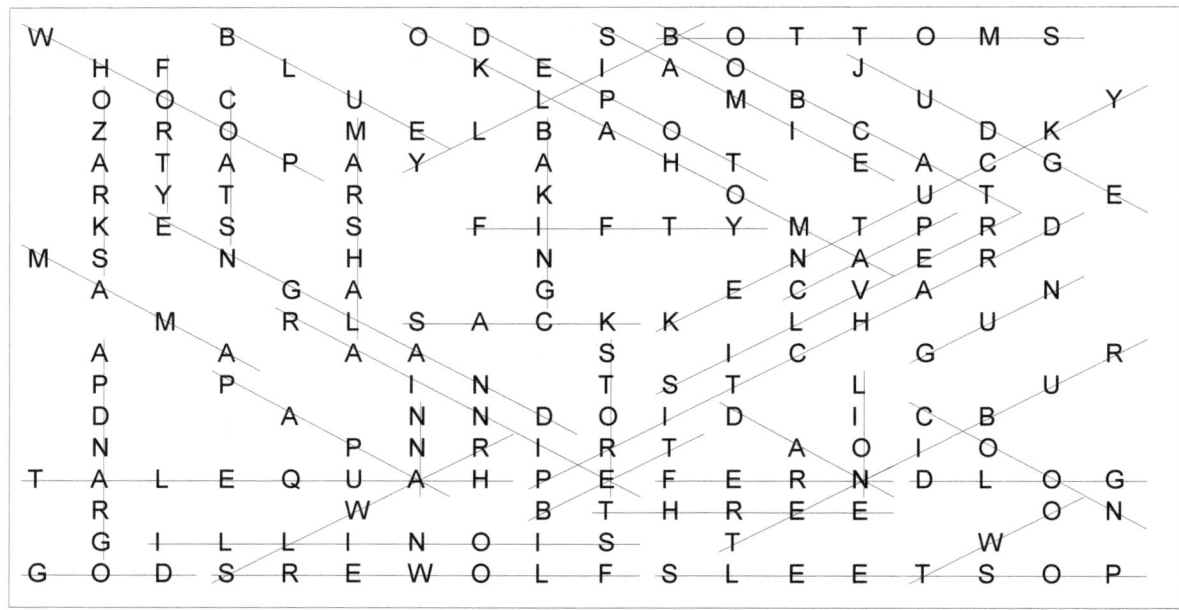

| ANN | COON | GOLD | OKLAHOMA | SAMIE |
| BAKING | DAN | GRANDPA | OZARKS | SILVER |
| BET | DEPOT | GUN | PAPA | SLEET |
| BILLY | ENGLAND | ILLINOIS | POST | STORE |
| BLUE | FERN | JUDGE | PRITCHARD | TALEQUAH |
| BOBCAT | FIFTY | KENTUCKY | RAINIE | TEN |
| BOTTOMS | FLOWERS | LION | RAWLS | THREE |
| CAP | FORTY | MAMA | RUBIN | TWO |
| COATS | GOD | MARSHAL | SACK | WHOOP |

Where The Red Fern Grows Word Search 4

Words are placed backwards, forward, diagonally, up and down. Words listed below are included in the maze. Circle the hidden vocabulary words in the maze.

```
F N N M O Z A R K S Y S I L V E R F
I R P P R P R I T C H A R D N N P G
F L S M M A R S H A L M J U D G E H
T G M M R P T P L P B I K X R L W T
Y C Y S N S O G K E X E J L I A N Q
Y L A Z O O R B R B E S T C N N R F
B I H P H A U Q E L A T W O G D E W
I O F W N S S S X Z O O C N T O F T
L N T D H C V F L P I R H T A F L V
L M P T H R E E E B L E E E I E E D
Y A E Q O U M D C O L P R S L R C N
L B P C L M L H R B I A O T K N T D
M C Z B Y B S D E C N P K G O D I V
S O R P M A Q I K A O A E U H R O B
A A U T Z K N N T I O E N W T N D
C T B R E I D N V J S N N M A M S
K S I M A N R A W L S R E W O L F D
T V N R V G K E N T U C K Y T R O F
```

| ANN | DAN | JUDGE | RINGTAIL |
| BAKING | DEPOT | KENTUCKY | RUBIN |
| BET | ENGLAND | LION | SACK |
| BILLY | FERN | MAMA | SAMIE |
| BLUE | FIFTY | MARSHAL | SILVER |
| BOBCAT | FLOWERS | OZARKS | SLEET |
| BOTTOMS | FORTY | PAPA | STORE |
| CAP | GOD | POST | TALEQUAH |
| CHEROKEE | GOLD | PRITCHARD | TEN |
| COATS | GRANDPA | RAINIE | THREE |
| CONTEST | GUN | RAWLS | TWO |
| COON | ILLINOIS | REFLECTION | WHOOP |

Where The Red Fern Grows Word Search 4 Answer Key

Words are placed backwards, forward, diagonally, up and down. Words listed below are included in the maze. Circle the hidden vocabulary words in the maze.

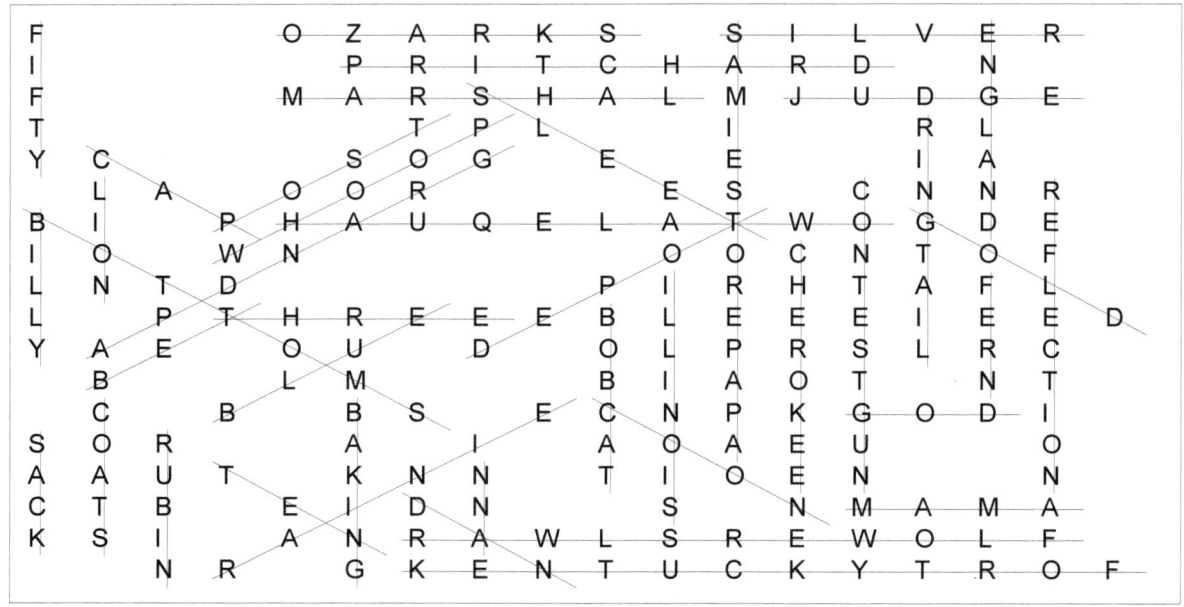

| ANN | DAN | JUDGE | RINGTAIL |
| BAKING | DEPOT | KENTUCKY | RUBIN |
| BET | ENGLAND | LION | SACK |
| BILLY | FERN | MAMA | SAMIE |
| BLUE | FIFTY | MARSHAL | SILVER |
| BOBCAT | FLOWERS | OZARKS | SLEET |
| BOTTOMS | FORTY | PAPA | STORE |
| CAP | GOD | POST | TALEQUAH |
| CHEROKEE | GOLD | PRITCHARD | TEN |
| COATS | GRANDPA | RAINIE | THREE |
| CONTEST | GUN | RAWLS | TWO |
| COON | ILLINOIS | REFLECTION | WHOOP |

Where The Red Fern Grows Crossword 1

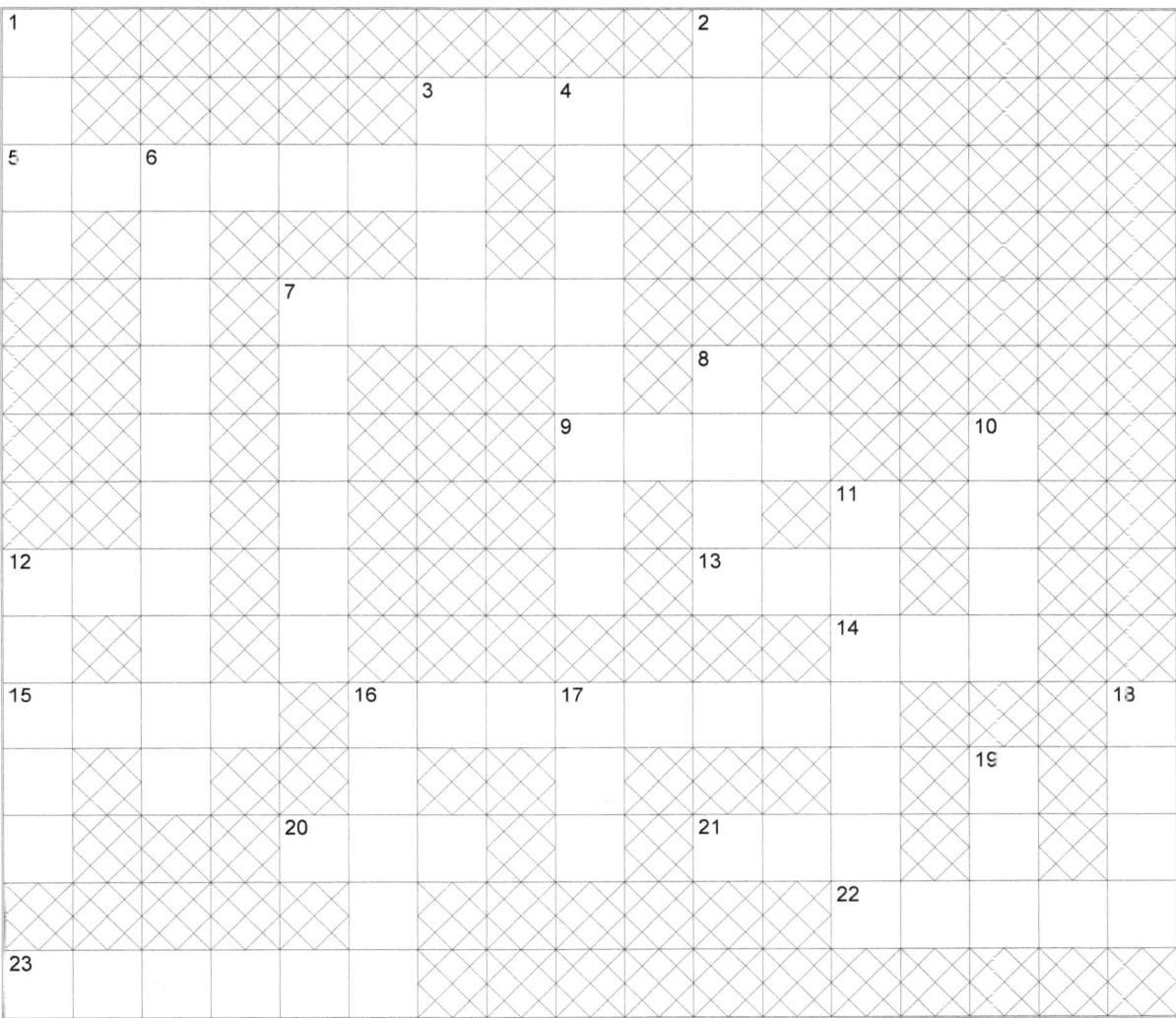

Across
3. Billy used a K.C. ___ Powder can for a bank
5. Rescued Billy from the fight with the town children
7. Weather during last night of the coon hunting contest
9. Billy didn't want to kill it: ghost ___
12. Grandpa made one with the Pritchard boys
13. Strong and aggressive: Old ___
14. Billy's other desire
15. Attacked Billy and the dogs: mountain ___
16. Nickname for a raccoon: Mr. ___
20. Dollar amount of Grandpa's bet with the Pritchard boys
21. Dollar amount Billy spent on gifts for the family
22. Where Billy picked up his puppies
23. Mountain setting of novel

Down
1. Prayed for a way to move to town
2. Smart but gun-shy: Little ___
3. The Pritchard's hound: Old ___
4. Location of kennel
6. Billy saw his for the first time on his trip to town
7. Cup Little Ann won at the beauty contest
8. Cup Billy gave to his youngest sister
10. Grew on a sacred spot: red ___
11. Where coonskin coat fad was: New ___
12. Was afflicted with puppy love
16. Author
17. Thought about and talked to frequently by Billy
18. Where the ghost coon hid: gate ___
19. Mama made one from Billy's first coon skin

Where The Red Fern Grows Crossword 1 Answer Key

|   | 1 M |   |   |   |   |   | 2 A |   |   |   |
|---|---|---|---|---|---|---|---|---|---|---|
|   | A |   |   | 3 B | 4 A | K | I | N | G |   |
| 5 M | A | R | S | H | A | L | L | E | N |   |
| A |   | E |   |   | U |   | N |   |   |   |
|   |   | F |   | 7 S | L | E | E | T |   |   |
|   |   | L |   | I |   |   |   | 8 G |   |   |
|   |   | E |   | L |   | 9 C | O | O | N | 10 F |
|   |   | C |   | V |   | K |   | L | 11 E | E |
| 12 B | E | T |   | E |   | Y |   | 13 D | A | N | R |
| I |   | I |   | R |   |   |   |   | 14 G | U | N |
| 15 L | I | O | N |   | 16 R | I | N | 17 G | T | A | I | L | 18 P |
| L |   | N |   |   | A |   |   | O |   |   | A | 19 C | O |
| Y |   |   |   | 20 T | W | O |   | D |   | 21 T | E | N | A | S |
|   |   |   |   | L |   |   |   |   |   |   | 22 D | E | P | O | T |
| 23 O | Z | A | R | K | S |   |   |   |   |   |   |   |   |   |

Across
3. Billy used a K.C. ___ Powder can for a bank
5. Rescued Billy from the fight with the town children
7. Weather during last night of the coon hunting contest
9. Billy didn't want to kill it: ghost ___
12. Grandpa made one with the Pritchard boys
13. Strong and aggressive: Old ___
14. Billy's other desire
15. Attacked Billy and the dogs: mountain ___
16. Nickname for a raccoon: Mr. ___
20. Dollar amount of Grandpa's bet with the Pritchard boys
21. Dollar amount Billy spent on gifts for the family
22. Where Billy picked up his puppies
23. Mountain setting of novel

Down
1. Prayed for a way to move to town
2. Smart but gun-shy: Little ___
3. The Pritchard's hound: Old ___
4. Location of kennel
6. Billy saw his for the first time on his trip to town
7. Cup Little Ann won at the beauty contest
8. Cup Billy gave to his youngest sister
10. Grew on a sacred spot: red ___
11. Where coonskin coat fad was: New ___
12. Was afflicted with puppy love
16. Author
17. Thought about and talked to frequently by Billy
18. Where the ghost coon hid: gate ___
19. Mama made one from Billy's first coon skin

# Where The Red Fern Grows Crossword 2

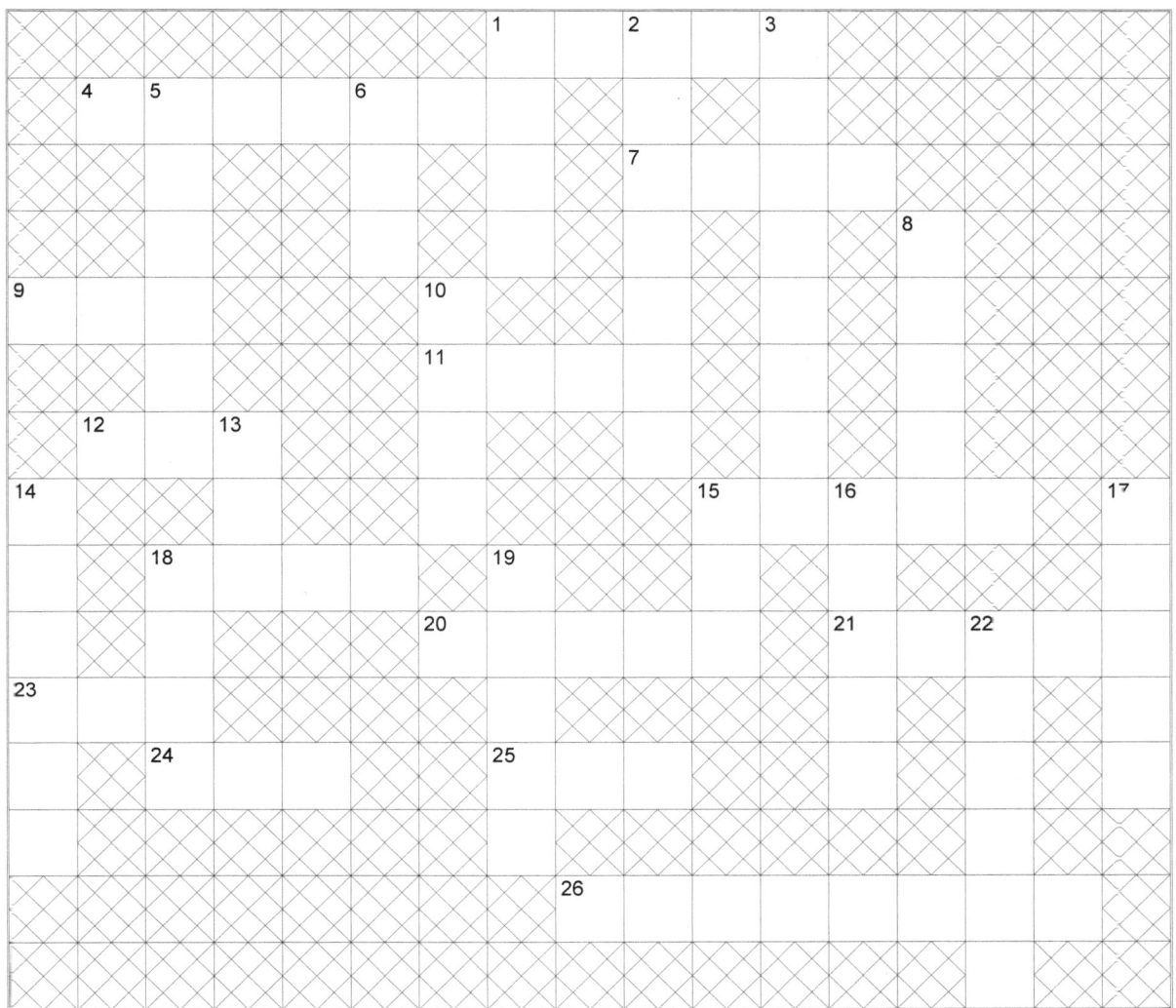

**Across**
1. Weather during last night of the coon hunting contest
4. Sent away for the dogs
7. Cup Billy gave to his youngest sister
9. Billy's other desire
11. Attacked Billy and the dogs: mountain ___
12. Grandpa made one with the Pritchard boys
15. Number of Billy's sisters
18. Where the ghost coon hid: gate ___
20. Fell on the axe and died
21. Sound Billy made to the hounds
23. Mama made one from Billy's first coon skin
24. Smart but gun-shy: Little ___
25. Thought about and talked to frequently by Billy
26. Location of kennel

**Down**
1. Billy carried the puppies home in one: gunny ___
2. Where coonskin coat fad was: New ___
3. Town Billy walked to for the dogs
5. Was excited on the hunt for the ghost coon
6. Strong and aggressive: Old ___
8. Where Grandpa worked
10. The Pritchard's hound: Old ___
13. Dollar amount of Grandpa's bet with the Pritchard boys
14. Billy thought the hounds had treed one
15. Dollar amount Billy spent on gifts for the family
16. Author
17. Where Billy picked up his puppies
18. Gave Billy three steel traps
19. Was amazed at Billy's dogs
22. Mountain setting of novel

Where The Red Fern Grows Crossword 2 Answer Key

|   |   |   |   |   |   | 1 S | 2 L | E | E | 3 T |   |   |   |
|---|---|---|---|---|---|---|---|---|---|---|---|---|---|
|   | 4 G | 5 R | A | N | 6 D | P | A |   | N |   | A |   |   |
|   |   | A |   |   | A |   | C |   | 7 G | O | L | D |   |
|   |   | I |   |   | N |   | K |   | L |   | E |   | 8 S |
| 9 G | U | N |   |   | 10 B |   | A |   | Q |   | T |   |   |
|   |   | I |   |   | 11 L | I | O | N |   | U |   | O |   |
|   | 12 B | E | 13 T |   | U |   | D |   | A |   | R |   |   |
| 14 B |   |   | W |   | E |   |   |   | 15 T | H | 16 R | E | E | 17 D |
| O |   | 18 P | O | S | T |   | 19 J |   | E |   | A |   |   | E |
| B |   | A |   |   | 20 R | U | B | I | N |   | 21 W | H | 22 O | O | P |
| 23 C | A | P |   |   |   |   | D |   |   |   | L |   | Z |   | O |
| A |   | 24 A | N | N |   | 25 G | O | D |   |   | S |   | A |   | T |
| T |   |   |   |   |   | E |   |   |   |   |   |   | R |   |   |
|   |   |   |   |   |   | 26 K | E | N | T | U | C | K | Y |   |   |
|   |   |   |   |   |   |   |   |   |   |   |   |   | S |   |   |

Across
1. Weather during last night of the coon hunting contest
4. Sent away for the dogs
7. Cup Billy gave to his youngest sister
9. Billy's other desire
11. Attacked Billy and the dogs: mountain ___
12. Grandpa made one with the Pritchard boys
15. Number of Billy's sisters
18. Where the ghost coon hid: gate ___
20. Fell on the axe and died
21. Sound Billy made to the hounds
23. Mama made one from Billy's first coon skin
24. Smart but gun-shy: Little ___
25. Thought about and talked to frequently by Billy
26. Location of kennel

Down
1. Billy carried the puppies home in one: gunny ___
2. Where coonskin coat fad was: New ___
3. Town Billy walked to for the dogs
5. Was excited on the hunt for the ghost coon
6. Strong and aggressive: Old ___
8. Where Grandpa worked
10. The Pritchard's hound: Old ___
13. Dollar amount of Grandpa's bet with the Pritchard boys
14. Billy thought the hounds had treed one
15. Dollar amount Billy spent on gifts for the family
16. Author
17. Where Billy picked up his puppies
18. Gave Billy three steel traps
19. Was amazed at Billy's dogs
22. Mountain setting of novel

# Where The Red Fern Grows Crossword 3

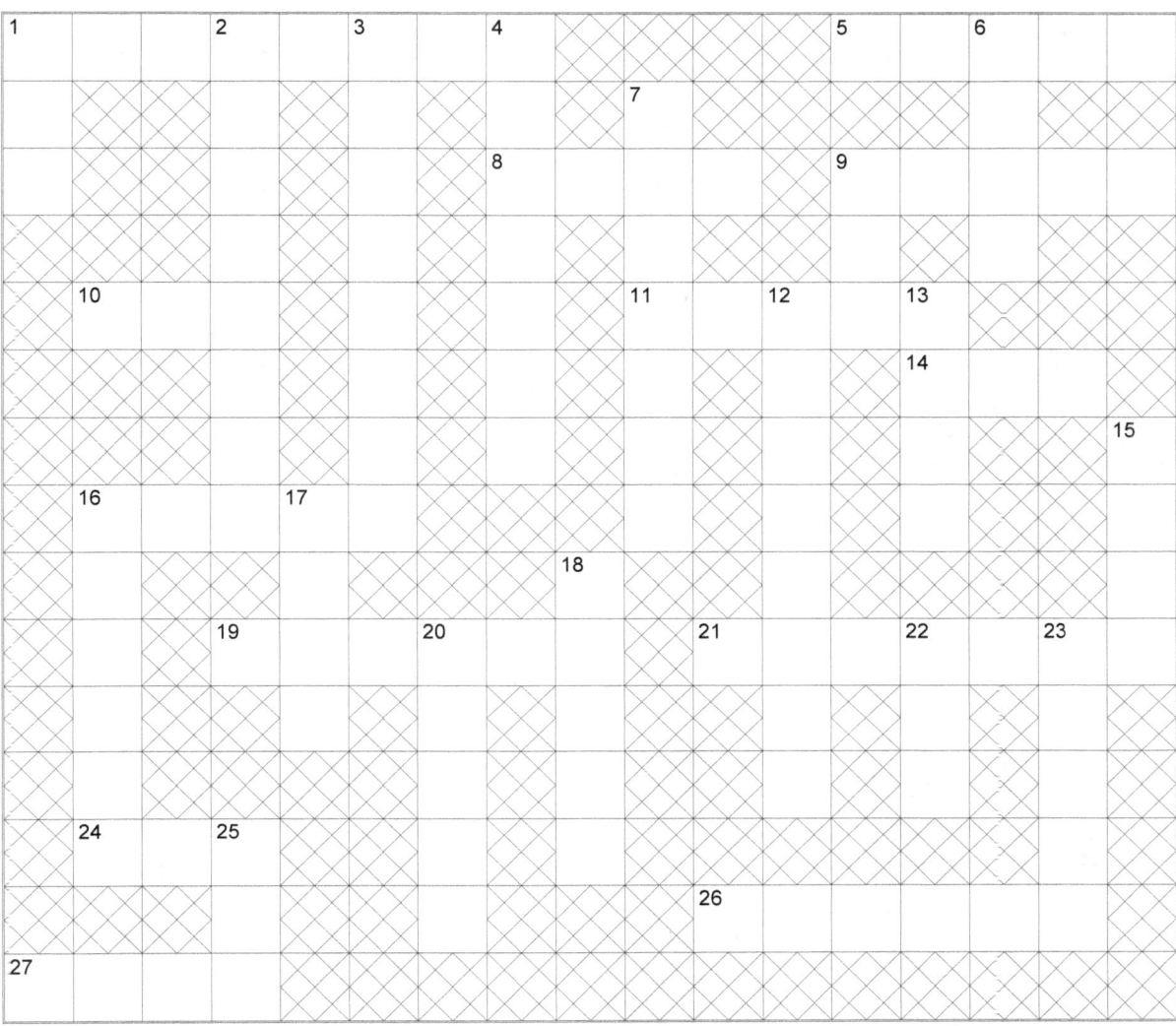

**Across**
1. Mama's Indian heritage
5. Dollar amount Billy saved
8. Cup Billy gave to his youngest sister
9. Number of Billy's sisters
10. Grandpa made one with the Pritchard boys
11. Sound Billy made to the hounds
14. Smart but gun-shy: Little ___
16. Was afflicted with puppy love
19. Billy thought the hounds had treed one
21. Grandpa entered the hounds in one
24. Thought about and talked to frequently by Billy
26. Was excited on the hunt for the ghost coon
27. Billy didn't want to kill it: ghost ___

**Down**
1. Mama made one from Billy's first coon skin
2. Nickname for a raccoon: Mr. ___
3. Location of kennel
4. Where coonskin coat fad was: New ___
6. Grew on a sacred spot: red ___
7. Billy put them on Rubin's grave
9. Dollar amount of Grandpa's bet with the Pritchard boys
12. State where Billy lived
13. Gave Billy three steel traps
15. Where the ghost coon hid: gate ___
16. Billy used a K.C. ___ Powder can for a bank
17. Attacked Billy and the dogs: mountain ___
18. Where Grandpa worked
20. Fad for coon skin ones raised the price of skins
22. Dollar amount Billy spent on gifts for the family
23. Curious cat
25. Strong and aggressive: Old ___

## Where The Red Fern Grows Crossword 3 Answer Key

|   | 1 C | H | 2 R | O | 3 K | E | 4 E |   |   | 5 F | 6 F | I | F | T | Y |
|---|---|---|---|---|---|---|---|---|---|---|---|---|---|---|---|
|   | A |   | I |   | E |   | N |   | 7 F |   | E |   |   |   |   |
|   | P |   | N |   | N |   | 8 G | O | L | D | 9 T | H | R | E | E |
|   |   |   | G |   | T |   | L |   | O |   | W |   | N |   |   |
|   |   | 10 B | E | T |   | U |   | A |   | 11 W | H | 12 O | O | 13 P |   |
|   |   |   | A |   | C |   | N |   | E |   | K |   | 14 A | N | N |
|   |   |   | I |   | K |   | D |   | R |   | L |   | P |   | 15 P |
|   |   | 16 B | I | 17 L | L | Y |   |   | S |   | A |   | A |   | O |
|   |   | A |   | I |   |   |   | 18 S |   |   | H |   |   |   | S |
|   |   | K |   | 19 B | O | 20 B | C | A | T |   | 21 C | O | 22 N | 23 T | E | S | T |
|   |   | I |   | N |   | O |   | O |   |   | M |   | E |   | A |
|   |   | N |   |   |   | A |   | R |   |   | A |   | N |   | M |
|   |   | 24 G | O | 25 D |   | T |   | E |   |   |   |   |   |   | I |
|   |   |   |   | A |   | S |   |   |   | 26 R | A | I | N | I | E |
| 27 C | O | O | N |   |   |   |   |   |   |   |   |   |   |   |   |

Across
1. Mama's Indian heritage
5. Dollar amount Billy saved
8. Cup Billy gave to his youngest sister
9. Number of Billy's sisters
10. Grandpa made one with the Pritchard boys
11. Sound Billy made to the hounds
14. Smart but gun-shy: Little ___
16. Was afflicted with puppy love
19. Billy thought the hounds had treed one
21. Grandpa entered the hounds in one
24. Thought about and talked to frequently by Billy
26. Was excited on the hunt for the ghost coon
27. Billy didn't want to kill it: ghost ___

Down
1. Mama made one from Billy's first coon skin
2. Nickname for a raccoon: Mr. __
3. Location of kennel
4. Where coonskin coat fad was: New ___
6. Grew on a sacred spot: red ___
7. Billy put them on Rubin's grave
9. Dollar amount of Grandpa's bet with the Pritchard boys
12. State where Billy lived
13. Gave Billy three steel traps
15. Where the ghost coon hid: gate ___
16. Billy used a K.C.___Powder can for a bank
17. Attacked Billy and the dogs: mountain ___
18. Where Grandpa worked
20. Fad for coon skin ones raised the price of skins
22. Dollar amount Billy spent on gifts for the family
23. Curious cat
25. Strong and aggressive: Old ___

# Where The Red Fern Grows Crossword 4

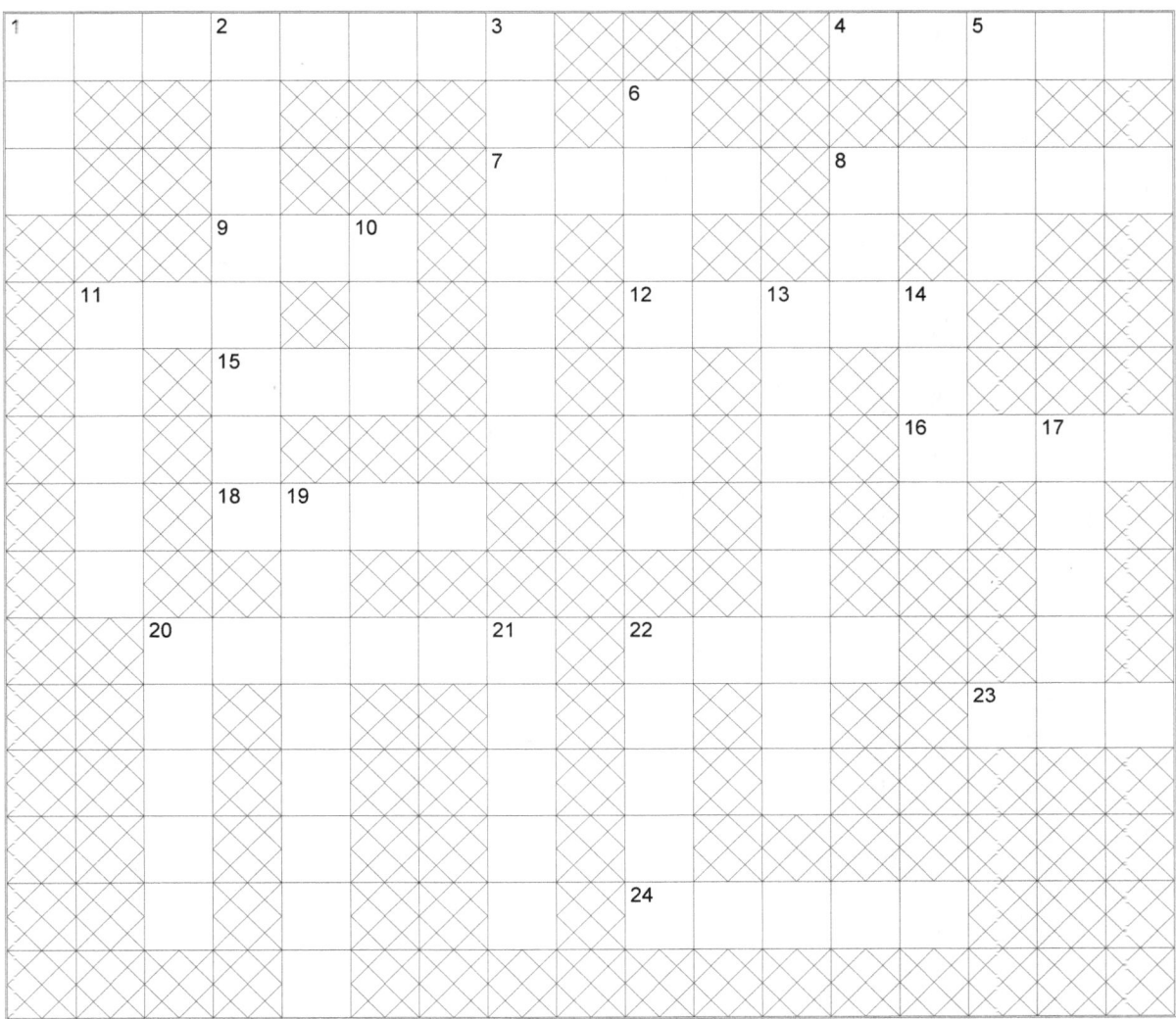

**Across**
1. Mama's Indian heritage
4. Dollar amount Billy saved
7. Cup Billy gave to his youngest sister
8. Number of Billy's sisters
9. Thought about and talked to frequently by Billy
11. Grandpa made one with the Pritchard boys
12. Sound Billy made to the hounds
15. Smart but gun-shy: Little ___
16. Where the ghost coon hid: gate ___
18. Attacked Billy and the dogs: mountain ___
20. Cup Little Ann won at the beauty contest
22. Billy didn't want to kill it: ghost ___
23. Dollar amount Billy spent on gifts for the family
24. Weather during last night of the coon hunting contest

**Down**
1. Mama made one from Billy's first coon skin
2. Nickname for a raccoon: Mr. ___
3. Where coonskin coat fad was: New ___
5. Grew on a sacred spot: red ___
6. Billy put them on Rubin's grave
8. Dollar amount of Grandpa's bet with the Pritchard boys
10. Strong and aggressive: Old ___
11. Was afflicted with puppy love
13. State where Billy lived
14. Gave Billy three steel traps
17. Where Grandpa worked
19. River near the bottoms
20. Curious cat
21. Author
22. Fad for coon skin ones raised the price of skins

Where The Red Fern Grows Crossword 4 Answer Key

|   | 1 C | H | 2 E R | O | K | E | 3 E |   |   | 4 F | 5 F | T | Y |
|---|---|---|---|---|---|---|---|---|---|---|---|---|---|
|   | A |   | I |   |   |   | N | 6 F |   |   | E |   |   |
|   | P |   | N |   |   |   | 7 G | O | L | D | 8 T | H | R | E | E |
|   |   |   |   | 9 G | 10 D |   | L | O |   |   | W |   | N |   |
|   | 11 B | E | T |   | A |   | A | 12 W | H | 13 O | 14 O | P |   |
|   | I |   | 15 A | N | N |   | N | E |   | K | A |   |   |
|   | L |   | I |   |   |   | D | R |   | L | 16 P | O | 17 S | T |
|   | L |   | 18 L | 19 I | O | N |   | S |   | A | A |   | T |
|   | Y |   |   | L |   |   |   |   |   | H |   |   | O |
|   |   | 20 S | I | L | V | E | 21 R |   | 22 C | O | O | N |   | R |
|   |   | A |   | I |   |   | A |   | O |   | M |   | 23 T | E | N |
|   |   | M |   | N |   |   | W |   | A |   | A |   |   |
|   |   | I |   | O |   |   | L |   | T |   |   |   |
|   |   | E |   | I |   |   | S |   | 24 S | L | E | E | T |
|   |   |   |   | S |   |   |   |   |   |   |   |   |   |

Across
1. Mama's Indian heritage
4. Dollar amount Billy saved
7. Cup Billy gave to his youngest sister
8. Number of Billy's sisters
9. Thought about and talked to frequently by Billy
11. Grandpa made one with the Pritchard boys
12. Sound Billy made to the hounds
15. Smart but gun-shy: Little ___
16. Where the ghost coon hid: gate ___
18. Attacked Billy and the dogs: mountain ___
20. Cup Little Ann won at the beauty contest
22. Billy didn't want to kill it: ghost ___
23. Dollar amount Billy spent on gifts for the family
24. Weather during last night of the coon hunting contest

Down
1. Mama made one from Billy's first coon skin
2. Nickname for a raccoon: Mr. ___
3. Where coonskin coat fad was: New ___
5. Grew on a sacred spot: red ___
6. Billy put them on Rubin's grave
8. Dollar amount of Grandpa's bet with the Pritchard boys
10. Strong and aggressive: Old ___
11. Was afflicted with puppy love
13. State where Billy lived
14. Gave Billy three steel traps
17. Where Grandpa worked
19. River near the bottoms
20. Curious cat
21. Author
22. Fad for coon skin ones raised the price of skins

Where The Red Fern Grows

| MAMA | BLUE | TEN | COATS | CHEROKEE |
|---|---|---|---|---|
| CAP | RAINIE | RINGTAIL | CONTEST | WHOOP |
| STORE | BOTTOMS | FREE SPACE | FORTY | JUDGE |
| PAPA | GOD | RAWLS | GUN | POST |
| SAMIE | GRANDPA | BET | RUBIN | PRITCHARD |

Where The Red Fern Grows

| ILLINOIS | FLOWERS | TWO | KENTUCKY | SACK |
|---|---|---|---|---|
| BILLY | OKLAHOMA | DEPOT | FERN | DAN |
| SLEET | BAKING | FREE SPACE | MARSHAL | ENGLAND |
| LION | FIFTY | THREE | REFLECTION | OZARKS |
| COON | TALEQUAH | GOLD | BOBCAT | PRITCHARD |

Where The Red Fern Grows

| POST | PAPA | BILLY | DAN | GOLD |
|---|---|---|---|---|
| BET | REFLECTION | GRANDPA | BAKING | RUBIN |
| BLUE | LION | FREE SPACE | SILVER | CAP |
| BOBCAT | DEPOT | BOTTOMS | SAMIE | SACK |
| PRITCHARD | STORE | TEN | ENGLAND | RINGTAIL |

Where The Red Fern Grows

| CHEROKEE | WHOOP | FIFTY | COON | THREE |
|---|---|---|---|---|
| FERN | SLEET | CONTEST | RAWLS | OZARKS |
| KENTUCKY | RAINIE | FREE SPACE | GUN | MARSHAL |
| COATS | OKLAHOMA | ILLINOIS | TALEQUAH | GOD |
| ANN | FLOWERS | JUDGE | MAMA | RINGTAIL |

Where The Red Fern Grows

| ENGLAND | JUDGE | GOLD | FERN | CAP |
|---|---|---|---|---|
| BILLY | COATS | WHOOP | BOTTOMS | ANN |
| TALEQUAH | BOBCAT | FREE SPACE | SLEET | TEN |
| SILVER | RAINIE | OZARKS | REFLECTION | DEPOT |
| PAPA | LION | RAWLS | FLOWERS | BET |

Where The Red Fern Grows

| FORTY | GOD | RINGTAIL | COON | STORE |
|---|---|---|---|---|
| TWO | BAKING | FIFTY | GRANDPA | SACK |
| CHEROKEE | CONTEST | FREE SPACE | PRITCHARD | DAN |
| ILLINOIS | RUBIN | THREE | MAMA | POST |
| BLUE | GUN | MARSHAL | SAMIE | BET |

Where The Red Fern Grows

| CHEROKEE | JUDGE | FIFTY | FLOWERS | BILLY |
|---|---|---|---|---|
| GUN | BAKING | RUBIN | PAPA | RAINIE |
| SACK | COATS | FREE SPACE | PRITCHARD | SILVER |
| TALEQUAH | GRANDPA | MAMA | LION | THREE |
| TEN | BOTTOMS | BET | DEPOT | REFLECTION |

Where The Red Fern Grows

| STORE | RINGTAIL | BOBCAT | OZARKS | CONTEST |
|---|---|---|---|---|
| OKLAHOMA | RAWLS | KENTUCKY | ANN | BLUE |
| FORTY | ILLINOIS | FREE SPACE | FERN | WHOOP |
| POST | ENGLAND | CAP | GOLD | MARSHAL |
| SLEET | DAN | SAMIE | GOD | REFLECTION |

Where The Red Fern Grows

| BLUE | DAN | PAPA | BOBCAT | WHOOP |
|---|---|---|---|---|
| GUN | SACK | RINGTAIL | RAINIE | MAMA |
| OZARKS | TALEQUAH | FREE SPACE | RAWLS | STORE |
| POST | MARSHAL | FIFTY | DEPOT | BET |
| BAKING | GOLD | CONTEST | TWO | RUBIN |

Where The Red Fern Grows

| CHEROKEE | SILVER | SLEET | BOTTOMS | SAMIE |
|---|---|---|---|---|
| COATS | REFLECTION | FORTY | ILLINOIS | OKLAHOMA |
| JUDGE | LION | FREE SPACE | ENGLAND | GOD |
| PRITCHARD | FLOWERS | FERN | COON | THREE |
| CAP | TEN | BILLY | KENTUCKY | RUBIN |

## Where The Red Fern Grows

| | | | | |
|---|---|---|---|---|
| SILVER | COATS | BET | CONTEST | COON |
| RAINIE | REFLECTION | FLOWERS | FIFTY | ILLINOIS |
| WHOOP | RUBIN | FREE SPACE | RAWLS | PAPA |
| GOLD | GUN | BILLY | BOBCAT | ENGLAND |
| CAP | JUDGE | ANN | OZARKS | DEPOT |

## Where The Red Fern Grows

| | | | | |
|---|---|---|---|---|
| KENTUCKY | BAKING | PRITCHARD | SACK | LION |
| CHEROKEE | SLEET | TWO | TEN | SAMIE |
| RINGTAIL | TALEQUAH | FREE SPACE | MAMA | FERN |
| OKLAHOMA | POST | THREE | GRANDPA | BOTTOMS |
| GOD | FORTY | DAN | STORE | DEPOT |

## Where The Red Fern Grows

| GUN | PAPA | OZARKS | SLEET | BET |
|---|---|---|---|---|
| RINGTAIL | ENGLAND | LION | DEPOT | THREE |
| COON | FERN | FREE SPACE | SACK | STORE |
| BAKING | PRITCHARD | TEN | GOLD | JUDGE |
| BOBCAT | KENTUCKY | BOTTOMS | GOD | TALEQUAH |

## Where The Red Fern Grows

| GRANDPA | SAMIE | ILLINOIS | RAWLS | DAN |
|---|---|---|---|---|
| CHEROKEE | RAINIE | CONTEST | POST | OKLAHOMA |
| MARSHAL | CAP | FREE SPACE | ANN | RUBIN |
| SILVER | BILLY | COATS | FORTY | WHOOP |
| TWO | MAMA | FIFTY | FLOWERS | TALEQUAH |

Where The Red Fern Grows

| BOBCAT | BILLY | GOLD | COON | FLOWERS |
|---|---|---|---|---|
| OZARKS | PAPA | WHOOP | BOTTOMS | POST |
| LION | RUBIN | FREE SPACE | TEN | ANN |
| OKLAHOMA | PRITCHARD | RAINIE | BET | TALEQUAH |
| THREE | SLEET | DEPOT | COATS | MARSHAL |

Where The Red Fern Grows

| FORTY | REFLECTION | BLUE | RINGTAIL | ILLINOIS |
|---|---|---|---|---|
| DAN | FIFTY | GOD | TWO | ENGLAND |
| FERN | SAMIE | FREE SPACE | GRANDPA | CAP |
| SACK | JUDGE | BAKING | GUN | RAWLS |
| KENTUCKY | STORE | CHEROKEE | CONTEST | MARSHAL |

Where The Red Fern Grows

| LION | KENTUCKY | GRANDPA | JUDGE | RUBIN |
|------|----------|---------|-------|-------|
| TEN | PRITCHARD | TALEQUAH | THREE | RAINIE |
| BET | BAKING | FREE SPACE | SILVER | SLEET |
| POST | MARSHAL | ENGLAND | WHOOP | FIFTY |
| DEPOT | RAWLS | TWO | BOTTOMS | ILLINOIS |

Where The Red Fern Grows

| REFLECTION | BILLY | CHEROKEE | CONTEST | COATS |
|------------|-------|----------|---------|-------|
| SAMIE | BLUE | GOD | OZARKS | ANN |
| GOLD | FLOWERS | FREE SPACE | MAMA | DAN |
| GUN | OKLAHOMA | PAPA | SACK | CAP |
| FORTY | BOBCAT | FERN | STORE | ILLINOIS |

Where The Red Fern Grows

| ENGLAND | MAMA | CHEROKEE | REFLECTION | GUN |
|---|---|---|---|---|
| WHOOP | RAWLS | OZARKS | RINGTAIL | KENTUCKY |
| GOD | BILLY | FREE SPACE | SAMIE | DAN |
| FIFTY | BOTTOMS | FERN | ANN | PAPA |
| GRANDPA | POST | SILVER | MARSHAL | FLOWERS |

Where The Red Fern Grows

| CAP | BLUE | DEPOT | BOBCAT | RUBIN |
|---|---|---|---|---|
| SACK | BET | FORTY | OKLAHOMA | TALEQUAH |
| PRITCHARD | LION | FREE SPACE | TWO | GOLD |
| RAINIE | BAKING | CONTEST | JUDGE | STORE |
| COON | COATS | ILLINOIS | SLEET | FLOWERS |

Where The Red Fern Grows

| ANN | GUN | FERN | MARSHAL | RINGTAIL |
|---|---|---|---|---|
| THREE | GOD | ENGLAND | WHOOP | OZARKS |
| CONTEST | DEPOT | FREE SPACE | DAN | FIFTY |
| PAPA | GOLD | CHEROKEE | RUBIN | PRITCHARD |
| JUDGE | BOBCAT | SLEET | BLUE | SACK |

Where The Red Fern Grows

| BET | FORTY | SAMIE | BILLY | TWO |
|---|---|---|---|---|
| STORE | CAP | COON | LION | GRANDPA |
| BAKING | REFLECTION | FREE SPACE | BOTTOMS | FLOWERS |
| MAMA | ILLINOIS | SILVER | RAWLS | RAINIE |
| POST | KENTUCKY | COATS | TALEQUAH | SACK |

Where The Red Fern Grows

| GUN | ILLINOIS | COON | LION | OZARKS |
|---|---|---|---|---|
| RINGTAIL | CONTEST | RAINIE | STORE | SILVER |
| GRANDPA | GOD | FREE SPACE | BOBCAT | MARSHAL |
| MAMA | SLEET | DAN | BLUE | TEN |
| COATS | JUDGE | TWO | RUBIN | SAMIE |

Where The Red Fern Grows

| BAKING | RAWLS | TALEQUAH | CAP | BET |
|---|---|---|---|---|
| FLOWERS | WHOOP | ANN | THREE | REFLECTION |
| PRITCHARD | ENGLAND | FREE SPACE | FIFTY | OKLAHOMA |
| PAPA | BILLY | POST | FERN | FORTY |
| DEPOT | BOTTOMS | SACK | GOLD | SAMIE |

### Where The Red Fern Grows

| | | | | |
|---|---|---|---|---|
| COON | TALEQUAH | JUDGE | LION | MARSHAL |
| TEN | DEPOT | SACK | OKLAHOMA | GOD |
| BAKING | REFLECTION | FREE SPACE | GRANDPA | POST |
| COATS | CONTEST | DAN | ILLINOIS | PAPA |
| WHOOP | FORTY | CHEROKEE | RAWLS | BET |

### Where The Red Fern Grows

| | | | | |
|---|---|---|---|---|
| BOBCAT | RUBIN | STORE | SILVER | BLUE |
| FIFTY | GOLD | SLEET | MAMA | FERN |
| GUN | ENGLAND | FREE SPACE | RINGTAIL | BILLY |
| CAP | FLOWERS | PRITCHARD | OZARKS | SAMIE |
| KENTUCKY | ANN | RAINIE | THREE | BET |

## Where The Red Fern Grows

| | | | | |
|---|---|---|---|---|
| COON | GOLD | JUDGE | TWO | FLOWERS |
| CHEROKEE | TEN | PRITCHARD | COATS | LION |
| ANN | GRANDPA | FREE SPACE | SAMIE | TALEQUAH |
| BOTTOMS | CAP | BLUE | RINGTAIL | FORTY |
| WHOOP | BILLY | DEPOT | ILLINOIS | FIFTY |

## Where The Red Fern Grows

| | | | | |
|---|---|---|---|---|
| RAWLS | POST | RUBIN | BET | OZARKS |
| DAN | REFLECTION | MARSHAL | STORE | KENTUCKY |
| ENGLAND | SLEET | FREE SPACE | THREE | BAKING |
| RAINIE | PAPA | SILVER | GUN | GOD |
| SACK | CONTEST | FERN | MAMA | FIFTY |

Where The Red Fern Grows

| BOTTOMS | STORE | FIFTY | GOLD | CHEROKEE |
|---|---|---|---|---|
| ANN | DAN | JUDGE | MAMA | BLUE |
| KENTUCKY | SILVER | FREE SPACE | DEPOT | TWO |
| BOBCAT | POST | THREE | MARSHAL | BET |
| OZARKS | COATS | WHOOP | FLOWERS | RINGTAIL |

Where The Red Fern Grows

| RUBIN | BAKING | GUN | CONTEST | ENGLAND |
|---|---|---|---|---|
| FERN | CAP | REFLECTION | SAMIE | OKLAHOMA |
| GOD | ILLINOIS | FREE SPACE | BILLY | PAPA |
| GRANDPA | PRITCHARD | RAWLS | LION | RAINIE |
| SLEET | SACK | TALEQUAH | FORTY | RINGTAIL |

Where The Red Fern Grows

| PRITCHARD | BOBCAT | SACK | STORE | FERN |
|---|---|---|---|---|
| COON | BOTTOMS | KENTUCKY | SILVER | CAP |
| DAN | MAMA | FREE SPACE | BLUE | RAINIE |
| CONTEST | RINGTAIL | BAKING | SLEET | LION |
| BILLY | POST | ILLINOIS | CHEROKEE | MARSHAL |

Where The Red Fern Grows

| GUN | BET | RAWLS | DEPOT | SAMIE |
|---|---|---|---|---|
| ANN | ENGLAND | COATS | TALEQUAH | GOLD |
| GOD | RUBIN | FREE SPACE | FLOWERS | FORTY |
| THREE | GRANDPA | OKLAHOMA | JUDGE | REFLECTION |
| FIFTY | TWO | OZARKS | PAPA | MARSHAL |

**Where The Red Fern Grows Vocabulary Word List**

| No. | Word | Clue/Definition |
|---|---|---|
| 1. | ASTONISHED | Filled with sudden wonder or amazement |
| 2. | BAWL | Crying or sobbing loudly; wailing |
| 3. | BAYING | Uttering a deep, prolonged bark |
| 4. | BEGRUDGINGLY | Reluctantly |
| 5. | BELLIGERENT | Inclined to fight; hostile or aggressive |
| 6. | BERSERK | Destructively or frenetically violent |
| 7. | BUSTLING | Moving energetically and busily |
| 8. | CARESS | A gentle touch or gesture of fondness, tenderness, or love |
| 9. | CLEAVED | Pierced or penetrated |
| 10. | COAXING | Persuading or trying to persuade by pleading or flattery |
| 11. | COMMOTION | An agitated disturbance |
| 12. | CONVENIENT | Easy to reach; accessible |
| 13. | DANGLING | Hanging loosely or swinging |
| 14. | DAZED | Stunned |
| 15. | DEFIANT | Boldly resisting |
| 16. | DEPOT | Railroad or bus station |
| 17. | DISLODGED | Removed or forced out from a position or dwelling |
| 18. | DOMAIN | Territory over which rule or control is exercised |
| 19. | DORMANT | Latent but capable of being activated; sleeping |
| 20. | DOUSED | Put out; extinguished |
| 21. | DRASTIC | Severe or radical in nature; extreme |
| 22. | DUMBFOUNDED | Filled with astonishment and perplexity |
| 23. | EAVES | Projecting overhang at the lower edge of a roof |
| 24. | EERIE | Strange and frightening |
| 25. | GINGERLY | With great care or delicacy; cautiously |
| 26. | GLOATED | Expressed great, often malicious, pleasure or self-satisfaction |
| 27. | GNAWING | Afflicting or worrying persistently |
| 28. | GRIEVE | Cause to be sorrowful; distress |
| 29. | GULLY | Deep ditch or channel cut in the earth by running water |
| 30. | HAMPERING | Preventing the free movement, action, or progress of |
| 31. | KEEN | Having a fine, sharp cutting edge or point |
| 32. | LIMBER | Bending or flexing readily; pliable |
| 33. | LITHE | Marked by effortless grace |
| 34. | LULL | A relatively calm interval |
| 35. | LUNGE | Sudden forward movement or plunge |
| 36. | MANTEL | Protruding shelf over a fireplace |
| 37. | MULLED | Gone over extensively in the mind |
| 38. | NONCHALANTLY | Unconcerned or indifferently |
| 39. | NOTCHED | Made a V-shaped cut |
| 40. | NOTION | Mental image; idea or conception |
| 41. | NUZZLING | Gently rubbing or pushing against |
| 42. | OBSTACLE | One that opposes, stands in the way of, or holds up progress |
| 43. | PACE | The rate of speed at which something is done |
| 44. | PANGS | Sudden sharp spasms of pain |
| 45. | PECULIARITY | Notable or distinctive feature or characteristic |
| 46. | PREDATORY | Living by hunting |
| 47. | PREDICAMENT | Unpleasant or troublesome situation that is hard to get out of |
| 48. | PROBED | Explored; investigated |
| 49. | QUENCH | Satisfy |
| 50. | QUIVERED | Shook with a slight, rapid, tremulous movement |
| 51. | SCOURGE | Widespread, dreadful affliction and devastation |

**Where The Red Fern Grows Vocabulary Word List Continued**

| No. | Word | Clue/Definition |
|---|---|---|
| 52. | SLOUGH | Depression or hollow, usually filled with deep mud or mire |
| 53. | SOBER | Serious, grave, or solemn |
| 54. | SQUABBLE | Noisy quarrel, usually about a trivial matter |
| 55. | SQUALLING | Screaming or crying loudly and harshly |
| 56. | VERGE | The point beyond which an action is likely to begin |
| 57. | VICIOUS | Marked by an aggressive disposition; savage |
| 58. | WADDLE | Walk with short steps that tilt the body from side to side |
| 59. | WILEY | Cunning |
| 60. | WOE | Deep distress or misery, as from grief, wretchedness |

Where The Red Fern Grows Vocabulary Fill In The Blank 1

_____

_____

_____

_____

_____

_____

_____

_____

_____

_____

_____

_____

_____

_____

_____

_____

_____

_____

_____

_____

1. Depression or hollow, usually filled with deep mud or mire
2. Uttering a deep, prolonged bark
3. Filled with astonishment and perplexity
4. With great care or delicacy; cautiously
5. Satisfy
6. Deep distress or misery, as from grief, wretchedness
7. Latent but capable of being activated; sleeping
8. Cunning
9. Mental image; idea or conception
10. Explored; investigated
11. Projecting overhang at the lower edge of a roof
12. Persuading or trying to persuade by pleading or flattery
13. Pierced or penetrated
14. Bending or flexing readily; pliable
15. An agitated disturbance
16. Inclined to fight; hostile or aggressive
17. Afflicting or worrying persistently
18. Unconcerned or indifferently
19. Expressed great, often malicious, pleasure or self-satisfaction
20. Walk with short steps that tilt the body from side to side

Where The Red Fern Grows Vocabulary Fill In The Blank 1 Answer Key

|  | |  |
|---|---|---|
| SLOUGH | | 1. Depression or hollow, usually filled with deep mud or mire |
| BAYING | | 2. Uttering a deep, prolonged bark |
| DUMBFOUNDED | | 3. Filled with astonishment and perplexity |
| GINGERLY | | 4. With great care or delicacy; cautiously |
| QUENCH | | 5. Satisfy |
| WOE | | 6. Deep distress or misery, as from grief, wretchedness |
| DORMANT | | 7. Latent but capable of being activated; sleeping |
| WILEY | | 8. Cunning |
| NOTION | | 9. Mental image; idea or conception |
| PROBED | | 10. Explored; investigated |
| EAVES | | 11. Projecting overhang at the lower edge of a roof |
| COAXING | | 12. Persuading or trying to persuade by pleading or flattery |
| CLEAVED | | 13. Pierced or penetrated |
| LIMBER | | 14. Bending or flexing readily; pliable |
| COMMOTION | | 15. An agitated disturbance |
| BELLIGERENT | | 16. Inclined to fight; hostile or aggressive |
| GNAWING | | 17. Afflicting or worrying persistently |
| NONCHALANTLY | | 18. Unconcerned or indifferently |
| GLOATED | | 19. Expressed great, often malicious, pleasure or self-satisfaction |
| WADDLE | | 20. Walk with short steps that tilt the body from side to side |

Where The Red Fern Grows Vocabulary Fill In The Blank 2

_____  1. Deep distress or misery, as from grief, wretchedness

_____  2. Protruding shelf over a fireplace

_____  3. Cause to be sorrowful; distress

_____  4. A relatively calm interval

_____  5. Put out; extinguished

_____  6. Marked by effortless grace

_____  7. Gone over extensively in the mind

_____  8. Severe or radical in nature; extreme

_____  9. Shook with a slight, rapid, tremulous movement

_____  10. Removed or forced out from a position or dwelling

_____  11. Filled with sudden wonder or amazement

_____  12. Hanging loosely or swinging

_____  13. Easy to reach; accessible

_____  14. Crying or sobbing loudly; wailing

_____  15. Pierced or penetrated

_____  16. Having a fine, sharp cutting edge or point

_____  17. Strange and frightening

_____  18. Walk with short steps that tilt the body from side to side

_____  19. Sudden forward movement or plunge

_____  20. Cunning

Where The Red Fern Grows Vocabulary Fill In The Blank 2 Answer Key

|  |  |
|---|---|
| WOE | 1. Deep distress or misery, as from grief, wretchedness |
| MANTEL | 2. Protruding shelf over a fireplace |
| GRIEVE | 3. Cause to be sorrowful; distress |
| LULL | 4. A relatively calm interval |
| DOUSED | 5. Put out; extinguished |
| LITHE | 6. Marked by effortless grace |
| MULLED | 7. Gone over extensively in the mind |
| DRASTIC | 8. Severe or radical in nature; extreme |
| QUIVERED | 9. Shook with a slight, rapid, tremulous movement |
| DISLODGED | 10. Removed or forced out from a position or dwelling |
| ASTONISHED | 11. Filled with sudden wonder or amazement |
| DANGLING | 12. Hanging loosely or swinging |
| CONVENIENT | 13. Easy to reach; accessible |
| BAWL | 14. Crying or sobbing loudly; wailing |
| CLEAVED | 15. Pierced or penetrated |
| KEEN | 16. Having a fine, sharp cutting edge or point |
| EERIE | 17. Strange and frightening |
| WADDLE | 18. Walk with short steps that tilt the body from side to side |
| LUNGE | 19. Sudden forward movement or plunge |
| WILEY | 20. Cunning |

Where The Red Fern Grows Vocabulary Fill In The Blank 3

_____

_____

_____

_____

_____

_____

_____

_____

_____

_____

_____

_____

_____

_____

_____

_____

_____

_____

_____

_____

1. With great care or delicacy; cautiously
2. Cause to be sorrowful; distress
3. Walk with short steps that tilt the body from side to side
4. Persuading or trying to persuade by pleading or flattery
5. Hanging loosely or swinging
6. Railroad or bus station
7. Protruding shelf over a fireplace
8. Destructively or frenetically violent
9. Living by hunting
10. Mental image; idea or conception
11. Afflicting or worrying persistently
12. Inclined to fight; hostile or aggressive
13. Deep distress or misery, as from grief, wretchedness
14. Widespread, dreadful affliction and devastation
15. Marked by an aggressive disposition; savage
16. Expressed great, often malicious, pleasure or self-satisfaction
17. Easy to reach; accessible
18. The point beyond which an action is likely to begin
19. Severe or radical in nature; extreme
20. Gently rubbing or pushing against

Where The Red Fern Grows Vocabulary Fill In The Blank 3 Answer Key

| | |
|---|---|
| GINGERLY | 1. With great care or delicacy; cautiously |
| GRIEVE | 2. Cause to be sorrowful; distress |
| WADDLE | 3. Walk with short steps that tilt the body from side to side |
| COAXING | 4. Persuading or trying to persuade by pleading or flattery |
| DANGLING | 5. Hanging loosely or swinging |
| DEPOT | 6. Railroad or bus station |
| MANTEL | 7. Protruding shelf over a fireplace |
| BERSERK | 8. Destructively or frenetically violent |
| PREDATORY | 9. Living by hunting |
| NOTION | 10. Mental image; idea or conception |
| GNAWING | 11. Afflicting or worrying persistently |
| BELLIGERENT | 12. Inclined to fight; hostile or aggressive |
| WOE | 13. Deep distress or misery, as from grief, wretchedness |
| SCOURGE | 14. Widespread, dreadful affliction and devastation |
| VICIOUS | 15. Marked by an aggressive disposition; savage |
| GLOATED | 16. Expressed great, often malicious, pleasure or self-satisfaction |
| CONVENIENT | 17. Easy to reach; accessible |
| VERGE | 18. The point beyond which an action is likely to begin |
| DRASTIC | 19. Severe or radical in nature; extreme |
| NUZZLING | 20. Gently rubbing or pushing against |

Where The Red Fern Grows Vocabulary Fill In The Blank 4

_____

1. Destructively or frenetically violent
2. The point beyond which an action is likely to begin
3. Severe or radical in nature; extreme
4. Screaming or crying loudly and harshly
5. Made a V-shaped cut
6. Stunned
7. Latent but capable of being activated; sleeping
8. Pierced or penetrated
9. Explored; investigated
10. Protruding shelf over a fireplace
11. Removed or forced out from a position or dwelling
12. Shook with a slight, rapid, tremulous movement
13. Inclined to fight; hostile or aggressive
14. Preventing the free movement, action, or progress of
15. Deep distress or misery, as from grief, wretchedness
16. Afflicting or worrying persistently
17. Living by hunting
18. Notable or distinctive feature or characteristic
19. Persuading or trying to persuade by pleading or flattery
20. The rate of speed at which something is done

Where The Red Fern Grows Vocabulary Fill In The Blank 4 Answer Key

|  | |  |
|---|---|---|
| BERSERK | | 1. Destructively or frenetically violent |
| VERGE | | 2. The point beyond which an action is likely to begin |
| DRASTIC | | 3. Severe or radical in nature; extreme |
| SQUALLING | | 4. Screaming or crying loudly and harshly |
| NOTCHED | | 5. Made a V-shaped cut |
| DAZED | | 6. Stunned |
| DORMANT | | 7. Latent but capable of being activated; sleeping |
| CLEAVED | | 8. Pierced or penetrated |
| PROBED | | 9. Explored; investigated |
| MANTEL | | 10. Protruding shelf over a fireplace |
| DISLODGED | | 11. Removed or forced out from a position or dwelling |
| QUIVERED | | 12. Shook with a slight, rapid, tremulous movement |
| BELLIGERENT | | 13. Inclined to fight; hostile or aggressive |
| HAMPERING | | 14. Preventing the free movement, action, or progress of |
| WOE | | 15. Deep distress or misery, as from grief, wretchedness |
| GNAWING | | 16. Afflicting or worrying persistently |
| PREDATORY | | 17. Living by hunting |
| PECULIARITY | | 18. Notable or distinctive feature or characteristic |
| COAXING | | 19. Persuading or trying to persuade by pleading or flattery |
| PACE | | 20. The rate of speed at which something is done |

Where The Red Fern Grows Vocabulary Matching 1

___ 1. DEPOT
___ 2. CONVENIENT
___ 3. DAZED
___ 4. GRIEVE
___ 5. SQUALLING
___ 6. DANGLING
___ 7. PREDICAMENT
___ 8. LITHE
___ 9. NONCHALANTLY
___ 10. PREDATORY
___ 11. WADDLE
___ 12. VICIOUS
___ 13. BERSERK
___ 14. OBSTACLE
___ 15. MULLED
___ 16. DEFIANT
___ 17. DUMBFOUNDED
___ 18. PROBED
___ 19. HAMPERING
___ 20. COMMOTION
___ 21. GLOATED
___ 22. BEGRUDGINGLY
___ 23. NUZZLING
___ 24. DISLODGED
___ 25. PACE

A. Stunned
B. Explored; investigated
C. Gone over extensively in the mind
D. Railroad or bus station
E. Screaming or crying loudly and harshly
F. Destructively or frenetically violent
G. Hanging loosely or swinging
H. Unpleasant or troublesome situation that is hard to get out of
I. Boldly resisting
J. Walk with short steps that tilt the body from side to side
K. Removed or forced out from a position or dwelling
L. Preventing the free movement, action, or progress of
M. An agitated disturbance
N. Reluctantly
O. Marked by effortless grace
P. One that opposes, stands in the way of, or holds up progress
Q. Expressed great, often malicious, pleasure or self-satisfaction
R. Marked by an aggressive disposition; savage
S. Filled with astonishment and perplexity
T. Easy to reach; accessible
U. Gently rubbing or pushing against
V. Unconcerned or indifferently
W. The rate of speed at which something is done
X. Cause to be sorrowful; distress
Y. Living by hunting

Where The Red Fern Grows Vocabulary Matching 1 Answer Key

| | | | |
|---|---|---|---|
| D - 1. | DEPOT | A. | Stunned |
| T - 2. | CONVENIENT | B. | Explored; investigated |
| A - 3. | DAZED | C. | Gone over extensively in the mind |
| X - 4. | GRIEVE | D. | Railroad or bus station |
| E - 5. | SQUALLING | E. | Screaming or crying loudly and harshly |
| G - 6. | DANGLING | F. | Destructively or frenetically violent |
| H - 7. | PREDICAMENT | G. | Hanging loosely or swinging |
| O - 8. | LITHE | H. | Unpleasant or troublesome situation that is hard to get out of |
| V - 9. | NONCHALANTLY | I. | Boldly resisting |
| Y - 10. | PREDATORY | J. | Walk with short steps that tilt the body from side to side |
| J - 11. | WADDLE | K. | Removed or forced out from a position or dwelling |
| R - 12. | VICIOUS | L. | Preventing the free movement, action, or progress of |
| F - 13. | BERSERK | M. | An agitated disturbance |
| P - 14. | OBSTACLE | N. | Reluctantly |
| C - 15. | MULLED | O. | Marked by effortless grace |
| I - 16. | DEFIANT | P. | One that opposes, stands in the way of, or holds up progress |
| S - 17. | DUMBFOUNDED | Q. | Expressed great, often malicious, pleasure or self-satisfaction |
| B - 18. | PROBED | R. | Marked by an aggressive disposition; savage |
| L - 19. | HAMPERING | S. | Filled with astonishment and perplexity |
| M - 20. | COMMOTION | T. | Easy to reach; accessible |
| Q - 21. | GLOATED | U. | Gently rubbing or pushing against |
| N - 22. | BEGRUDGINGLY | V. | Unconcerned or indifferently |
| U - 23. | NUZZLING | W. | The rate of speed at which something is done |
| K - 24. | DISLODGED | X. | Cause to be sorrowful; distress |
| W - 25. | PACE | Y. | Living by hunting |

Where The Red Fern Grows Vocabulary Matching 2

___ 1. COAXING
___ 2. WILEY
___ 3. PACE
___ 4. MULLED
___ 5. DUMBFOUNDED
___ 6. SCOURGE
___ 7. DORMANT
___ 8. DEPOT
___ 9. SQUALLING
___10. QUENCH
___11. NUZZLING
___12. GULLY
___13. DISLODGED
___14. PANGS
___15. LIMBER
___16. PREDICAMENT
___17. GRIEVE
___18. PECULIARITY
___19. DOMAIN
___20. CARESS
___21. PROBED
___22. PREDATORY
___23. ASTONISHED
___24. MANTEL
___25. SLOUGH

A. Screaming or crying loudly and harshly
B. A gentle touch or gesture of fondness, tenderness, or love
C. Bending or flexing readily; pliable
D. Deep ditch or channel cut in the earth by running water
E. Railroad or bus station
F. Filled with astonishment and perplexity
G. Satisfy
H. Living by hunting
I. Gently rubbing or pushing against
J. Notable or distinctive feature or characteristic
K. Gone over extensively in the mind
L. Removed or forced out from a position or dwelling
M. Unpleasant or troublesome situation that is hard to get out of
N. Latent but capable of being activated; sleeping
O. Protruding shelf over a fireplace
P. Sudden sharp spasms of pain
Q. Widespread, dreadful affliction and devastation
R. Filled with sudden wonder or amazement
S. Cunning
T. Persuading or trying to persuade by pleading or flattery
U. Depression or hollow, usually filled with deep mud or mire
V. Territory over which rule or control is exercised
W. Cause to be sorrowful; distress
X. The rate of speed at which something is done
Y. Explored; investigated

Where The Red Fern Grows Vocabulary Matching 2 Answer Key

T - 1. COAXING — A. Screaming or crying loudly and harshly
S - 2. WILEY — B. A gentle touch or gesture of fondness, tenderness, or love
X - 3. PACE — C. Bending or flexing readily; pliable
K - 4. MULLED — D. Deep ditch or channel cut in the earth by running water
F - 5. DUMBFOUNDED — E. Railroad or bus station
Q - 6. SCOURGE — F. Filled with astonishment and perplexity
N - 7. DORMANT — G. Satisfy
E - 8. DEPOT — H. Living by hunting
A - 9. SQUALLING — I. Gently rubbing or pushing against
G - 10. QUENCH — J. Notable or distinctive feature or characteristic
I - 11. NUZZLING — K. Gone over extensively in the mind
D - 12. GULLY — L. Removed or forced out from a position or dwelling
L - 13. DISLODGED — M. Unpleasant or troublesome situation that is hard to get out of
P - 14. PANGS — N. Latent but capable of being activated; sleeping
C - 15. LIMBER — O. Protruding shelf over a fireplace
M - 16. PREDICAMENT — P. Sudden sharp spasms of pain
W - 17. GRIEVE — Q. Widespread, dreadful affliction and devastation
J - 18. PECULIARITY — R. Filled with sudden wonder or amazement
V - 19. DOMAIN — S. Cunning
B - 20. CARESS — T. Persuading or trying to persuade by pleading or flattery
Y - 21. PROBED — U. Depression or hollow, usually filled with deep mud or mire
H - 22. PREDATORY — V. Territory over which rule or control is exercised
R - 23. ASTONISHED — W. Cause to be sorrowful; distress
O - 24. MANTEL — X. The rate of speed at which something is done
U - 25. SLOUGH — Y. Explored; investigated

Where The Red Fern Grows Vocabulary Matching 3

___ 1. DUMBFOUNDED  A. Crying or sobbing loudly; wailing
___ 2. CONVENIENT  B. Walk with short steps that tilt the body from side to side
___ 3. DEFIANT  C. Mental image; idea or conception
___ 4. LULL  D. Satisfy
___ 5. CLEAVED  E. Hanging loosely or swinging
___ 6. DRASTIC  F. Uttering a deep, prolonged bark
___ 7. ASTONISHED  G. Afflicting or worrying persistently
___ 8. LIMBER  H. Bending or flexing readily; pliable
___ 9. WADDLE  I. Sudden forward movement or plunge
___10. DANGLING  J. Cunning
___11. QUIVERED  K. Pierced or penetrated
___12. GNAWING  L. Explored; investigated
___13. PREDICAMENT  M. Filled with astonishment and perplexity
___14. WILEY  N. Unpleasant or troublesome situation that is hard to get out of
___15. MULLED  O. Easy to reach; accessible
___16. SLOUGH  P. Filled with sudden wonder or amazement
___17. BAWL  Q. A relatively calm interval
___18. NOTION  R. Gone over extensively in the mind
___19. GINGERLY  S. Made a V-shaped cut
___20. QUENCH  T. Depression or hollow, usually filled with deep mud or mire
___21. PROBED  U. With great care or delicacy; cautiously
___22. LUNGE  V. Boldly resisting
___23. BAYING  W. Moving energetically and busily
___24. NOTCHED  X. Shook with a slight, rapid, tremulous movement
___25. BUSTLING  Y. Severe or radical in nature; extreme

Where The Red Fern Grows Vocabulary Matching 3 Answer Key

| | | |
|---|---|---|
| M - 1. | DUMBFOUNDED | A. Crying or sobbing loudly; wailing |
| O - 2. | CONVENIENT | B. Walk with short steps that tilt the body from side to side |
| V - 3. | DEFIANT | C. Mental image; idea or conception |
| Q - 4. | LULL | D. Satisfy |
| K - 5. | CLEAVED | E. Hanging loosely or swinging |
| Y - 6. | DRASTIC | F. Uttering a deep, prolonged bark |
| P - 7. | ASTONISHED | G. Afflicting or worrying persistently |
| H - 8. | LIMBER | H. Bending or flexing readily; pliable |
| B - 9. | WADDLE | I. Sudden forward movement or plunge |
| E - 10. | DANGLING | J. Cunning |
| X - 11. | QUIVERED | K. Pierced or penetrated |
| G - 12. | GNAWING | L. Explored; investigated |
| N - 13. | PREDICAMENT | M. Filled with astonishment and perplexity |
| J - 14. | WILEY | N. Unpleasant or troublesome situation that is hard to get out of |
| R - 15. | MULLED | O. Easy to reach; accessible |
| T - 16. | SLOUGH | P. Filled with sudden wonder or amazement |
| A - 17. | BAWL | Q. A relatively calm interval |
| C - 18. | NOTION | R. Gone over extensively in the mind |
| U - 19. | GINGERLY | S. Made a V-shaped cut |
| D - 20. | QUENCH | T. Depression or hollow, usually filled with deep mud or mire |
| L - 21. | PROBED | U. With great care or delicacy; cautiously |
| I - 22. | LUNGE | V. Boldly resisting |
| F - 23. | BAYING | W. Moving energetically and busily |
| S - 24. | NOTCHED | X. Shook with a slight, rapid, tremulous movement |
| W - 25. | BUSTLING | Y. Severe or radical in nature; extreme |

Where The Red Fern Grows Vocabulary Matching 4

___ 1. PREDICAMENT
___ 2. NONCHALANTLY
___ 3. DEPOT
___ 4. GULLY
___ 5. NOTION
___ 6. WOE
___ 7. SQUABBLE
___ 8. SLOUGH
___ 9. WADDLE
___ 10. DRASTIC
___ 11. QUIVERED
___ 12. VICIOUS
___ 13. CARESS
___ 14. EERIE
___ 15. CONVENIENT
___ 16. COMMOTION
___ 17. LUNGE
___ 18. PECULIARITY
___ 19. QUENCH
___ 20. HAMPERING
___ 21. VERGE
___ 22. SQUALLING
___ 23. BERSERK
___ 24. GNAWING
___ 25. PANGS

A. Unpleasant or troublesome situation that is hard to get out of
B. The point beyond which an action is likely to begin
C. Walk with short steps that tilt the body from side to side
D. Destructively or frenetically violent
E. Sudden sharp spasms of pain
F. Railroad or bus station
G. Afflicting or worrying persistently
H. Satisfy
I. An agitated disturbance
J. Sudden forward movement or plunge
K. Screaming or crying loudly and harshly
L. Mental image; idea or conception
M. Unconcerned or indifferently
N. Preventing the free movement, action, or progress of
O. Deep ditch or channel cut in the earth by running water
P. A gentle touch or gesture of fondness, tenderness, or love
Q. Easy to reach; accessible
R. Shook with a slight, rapid, tremulous movement
S. Depression or hollow, usually filled with deep mud or mire
T. Strange and frightening
U. Deep distress or misery, as from grief, wretchedness
V. Noisy quarrel, usually about a trivial matter
W. Notable or distinctive feature or characteristic
X. Severe or radical in nature; extreme
Y. Marked by an aggressive disposition; savage

Where The Red Fern Grows Vocabulary Matching 4 Answer Key

| | | | |
|---|---|---|---|
| A - 1. | PREDICAMENT | A. | Unpleasant or troublesome situation that is hard to get out of |
| M - 2. | NONCHALANTLY | B. | The point beyond which an action is likely to begin |
| F - 3. | DEPOT | C. | Walk with short steps that tilt the body from side to side |
| O - 4. | GULLY | D. | Destructively or frenetically violent |
| L - 5. | NOTION | E. | Sudden sharp spasms of pain |
| U - 6. | WOE | F. | Railroad or bus station |
| V - 7. | SQUABBLE | G. | Afflicting or worrying persistently |
| S - 8. | SLOUGH | H. | Satisfy |
| C - 9. | WADDLE | I. | An agitated disturbance |
| X - 10. | DRASTIC | J. | Sudden forward movement or plunge |
| R - 11. | QUIVERED | K. | Screaming or crying loudly and harshly |
| Y - 12. | VICIOUS | L. | Mental image; idea or conception |
| P - 13. | CARESS | M. | Unconcerned or indifferently |
| T - 14. | EERIE | N. | Preventing the free movement, action, or progress of |
| Q - 15. | CONVENIENT | O. | Deep ditch or channel cut in the earth by running water |
| I - 16. | COMMOTION | P. | A gentle touch or gesture of fondness, tenderness, or love |
| J - 17. | LUNGE | Q. | Easy to reach; accessible |
| W - 18. | PECULIARITY | R. | Shook with a slight, rapid, tremulous movement |
| H - 19. | QUENCH | S. | Depression or hollow, usually filled with deep mud or mire |
| N - 20. | HAMPERING | T. | Strange and frightening |
| B - 21. | VERGE | U. | Deep distress or misery, as from grief, wretchedness |
| K - 22. | SQUALLING | V. | Noisy quarrel, usually about a trivial matter |
| D - 23. | BERSERK | W. | Notable or distinctive feature or characteristic |
| G - 24. | GNAWING | X. | Severe or radical in nature; extreme |
| E - 25. | PANGS | Y. | Marked by an aggressive disposition; savage |

Where The Red Fern Grows Vocabulary Magic Squares 1

Match the definition with the vocabulary word. Put your answers in the magic squares below. When your answers are correct, all columns and rows will add to the same number.

A. PREDATORY
B. EERIE
C. SCOURGE
D. DEPOT
E. DOUSED
F. LITHE
G. EAVES
H. GULLY
I. VICIOUS
J. PACE
K. QUIVERED
L. SLOUGH
M. DAZED
N. PROBED
O. MANTEL
P. LIMBER

1. Living by hunting
2. Explored; investigated
3. The rate of speed at which something is done
4. Put out; extinguished
5. Projecting overhang at the lower edge of a roof
6. Depression or hollow, usually filled with deep mud or mire
7. Bending or flexing readily; pliable
8. Widespread, dreadful affliction and devastation
9. Protruding shelf over a fireplace
10. Railroad or bus station
11. Deep ditch or channel cut in the earth by running water
12. Shook with a slight, rapid, tremulous movement
13. Marked by an aggressive disposition; savage
14. Marked by effortless grace
15. Strange and frightening
16. Stunned

| A= | B= | C= | D= |
| E= | F= | G= | H= |
| I= | J= | K= | L= |
| M= | N= | O= | P= |

Where The Red Fern Grows Vocabulary Magic Squares 1 Answer Key

Match the definition with the vocabulary word. Put your answers in the magic squares below. When your answers are correct, all columns and rows will add to the same number.

A. PREDATORY
B. EERIE
C. SCOURGE
D. DEPOT
E. DOUSED
F. LITHE
G. EAVES
H. GULLY
I. VICIOUS
J. PACE
K. QUIVERED
L. SLOUGH
M. DAZED
N. PROBED
O. MANTEL
P. LIMBER

1. Living by hunting
2. Explored; investigated
3. The rate of speed at which something is done
4. Put out; extinguished
5. Projecting overhang at the lower edge of a roof
6. Depression or hollow, usually filled with deep mud or mire
7. Bending or flexing readily; pliable
8. Widespread, dreadful affliction and devastation
9. Protruding shelf over a fireplace
10. Railroad or bus station
11. Deep ditch or channel cut in the earth by running water
12. Shook with a slight, rapid, tremulous movement
13. Marked by an aggressive disposition; savage
14. Marked by effortless grace
15. Strange and frightening
16. Stunned

| A=1 | B=15 | C=8 | D=10 |
| --- | --- | --- | --- |
| E=4 | F=14 | G=5 | H=11 |
| I=13 | J=3 | K=12 | L=6 |
| M=16 | N=2 | O=9 | P=7 |

Where The Red Fern Grows Vocabulary Magic Squares 2

Match the definition with the vocabulary word. Put your answers in the magic squares below. When your answers are correct, all columns and rows will add to the same number.

A. PECULIARITY
B. NUZZLING
C. GRIEVE
D. SQUABBLE
E. BELLIGERENT
F. BERSERK
G. PACE
H. BEGRUDGINGLY
I. NONCHALANTLY
J. GINGERLY
K. QUIVERED
L. COMMOTION
M. BAWL
N. MANTEL
O. SQUALLING
P. BAYING

1. Reluctantly
2. Notable or distinctive feature or characteristic
3. Gently rubbing or pushing against
4. The rate of speed at which something is done
5. With great care or delicacy; cautiously
6. Screaming or crying loudly and harshly
7. Uttering a deep, prolonged bark
8. Unconcerned or indifferently
9. Shook with a slight, rapid, tremulous movement
10. Protruding shelf over a fireplace
11. Crying or sobbing loudly; wailing
12. An agitated disturbance
13. Inclined to fight; hostile or aggressive
14. Noisy quarrel, usually about a trivial matter
15. Cause to be sorrowful; distress
16. Destructively or frenetically violent

| A= | B= | C= | D= |
| E= | F= | G= | H= |
| I= | J= | K= | L= |
| M= | N= | O= | P= |

Where The Red Fern Grows Vocabulary Magic Squares 2 Answer Key

Match the definition with the vocabulary word. Put your answers in the magic squares below. When your answers are correct, all columns and rows will add to the same number.

A. PECULIARITY
B. NUZZLING
C. GRIEVE
D. SQUABBLE
E. BELLIGERENT
F. BERSERK
G. PACE
H. BEGRUDGINGLY
I. NONCHALANTLY
J. GINGERLY
K. QUIVERED
L. COMMOTION
M. BAWL
N. MANTEL
O. SQUALLING
P. BAYING

1. Reluctantly
2. Notable or distinctive feature or characteristic
3. Gently rubbing or pushing against
4. The rate of speed at which something is done
5. With great care or delicacy; cautiously
6. Screaming or crying loudly and harshly
7. Uttering a deep, prolonged bark
8. Unconcerned or indifferently
9. Shook with a slight, rapid, tremulous movement
10. Protruding shelf over a fireplace
11. Crying or sobbing loudly; wailing
12. An agitated disturbance
13. Inclined to fight; hostile or aggressive
14. Noisy quarrel, usually about a trivial matter
15. Cause to be sorrowful; distress
16. Destructively or frenetically violent

| A=2 | B=3 | C=15 | D=14 |
| --- | --- | --- | --- |
| E=13 | F=16 | G=4 | H=1 |
| I=8 | J=5 | K=9 | L=12 |
| M=11 | N=10 | O=6 | P=7 |

Where The Red Fern Grows Vocabulary Magic Squares 3

Match the definition with the vocabulary word. Put your answers in the magic squares below. When your answers are correct, all columns and rows will add to the same number.

A. LITHE
B. NOTCHED
C. EAVES
D. DISLODGED
E. PREDICAMENT
F. ASTONISHED
G. WADDLE
H. QUIVERED
I. CONVENIENT
J. BUSTLING
K. BEGRUDGINGLY
L. HAMPERING
M. PREDATORY
N. NUZZLING
O. QUENCH
P. NONCHALANTLY

1. Satisfy
2. Removed or forced out from a position or dwelling
3. Moving energetically and busily
4. Unpleasant or troublesome situation that is hard to get out of
5. Easy to reach; accessible
6. Filled with sudden wonder or amazement
7. Unconcerned or indifferently
8. Projecting overhang at the lower edge of a roof
9. Shook with a slight, rapid, tremulous movement
10. Reluctantly
11. Marked by effortless grace
12. Gently rubbing or pushing against
13. Made a V-shaped cut
14. Living by hunting
15. Walk with short steps that tilt the body from side to side
16. Preventing the free movement, action, or progress of

| A= | B= | C= | D= |
|---|---|---|---|
| E= | F= | G= | H= |
| I= | J= | K= | L= |
| M= | N= | O= | P= |

Where The Red Fern Grows Vocabulary Magic Squares 3 Answer Key

Match the definition with the vocabulary word. Put your answers in the magic squares below. When your answers are correct, all columns and rows will add to the same number.

A. LITHE
B. NOTCHED
C. EAVES
D. DISLODGED
E. PREDICAMENT
F. ASTONISHED
G. WADDLE
H. QUIVERED
I. CONVENIENT
J. BUSTLING
K. BEGRUDGINGLY
L. HAMPERING
M. PREDATORY
N. NUZZLING
O. QUENCH
P. NONCHALANTLY

1. Satisfy
2. Removed or forced out from a position or dwelling
3. Moving energetically and busily
4. Unpleasant or troublesome situation that is hard to get out of
5. Easy to reach; accessible
6. Filled with sudden wonder or amazement
7. Unconcerned or indifferently
8. Projecting overhang at the lower edge of a roof
9. Shook with a slight, rapid, tremulous movement
10. Reluctantly
11. Marked by effortless grace
12. Gently rubbing or pushing against
13. Made a V-shaped cut
14. Living by hunting
15. Walk with short steps that tilt the body from side to side
16. Preventing the free movement, action, or progress of

| A=11 | B=13 | C=8 | D=2 |
| --- | --- | --- | --- |
| E=4 | F=6 | G=15 | H=9 |
| I=5 | J=3 | K=10 | L=16 |
| M=14 | N=12 | O=1 | P=7 |

Where The Red Fern Grows Vocabulary Magic Squares 4

Match the definition with the vocabulary word. Put your answers in the magic squares below. When your answers are correct, all columns and rows will add to the same number.

A. EERIE
B. CONVENIENT
C. GNAWING
D. QUENCH
E. SOBER
F. GULLY
G. WILEY
H. NOTCHED
I. DOMAIN
J. MANTEL
K. BAWL
L. SCOURGE
M. GLOATED
N. VERGE
O. PANGS
P. CLEAVED

1. Made a V-shaped cut
2. Expressed great, often malicious, pleasure or self-satisfaction
3. Easy to reach; accessible
4. Crying or sobbing loudly; wailing
5. Protruding shelf over a fireplace
6. Afflicting or worrying persistently
7. Pierced or penetrated
8. Serious, grave, or solemn
9. Sudden sharp spasms of pain
10. Deep ditch or channel cut in the earth by running water
11. Territory over which rule or control is exercised
12. Satisfy
13. Strange and frightening
14. Widespread, dreadful affliction and devastation
15. Cunning
16. The point beyond which an action is likely to begin

| A= | B= | C= | D= |
|---|---|---|---|
| E= | F= | G= | H= |
| I= | J= | K= | L= |
| M= | N= | O= | P= |

Where The Red Fern Grows Vocabulary Magic Squares 4 Answer Key

Match the definition with the vocabulary word. Put your answers in the magic squares below. When your answers are correct, all columns and rows will add to the same number.

A. EERIE
B. CONVENIENT
C. GNAWING
D. QUENCH
E. SOBER
F. GULLY
G. WILEY
H. NOTCHED
I. DOMAIN
J. MANTEL
K. BAWL
L. SCOURGE
M. GLOATED
N. VERGE
O. PANGS
P. CLEAVED

1. Made a V-shaped cut
2. Expressed great, often malicious, pleasure or self-satisfaction
3. Easy to reach; accessible
4. Crying or sobbing loudly; wailing
5. Protruding shelf over a fireplace
6. Afflicting or worrying persistently
7. Pierced or penetrated
8. Serious, grave, or solemn
9. Sudden sharp spasms of pain
10. Deep ditch or channel cut in the earth by running water
11. Territory over which rule or control is exercised
12. Satisfy
13. Strange and frightening
14. Widespread, dreadful affliction and devastation
15. Cunning
16. The point beyond which an action is likely to begin

| A=13 | B=3  | C=6  | D=12 |
|------|------|------|------|
| E=8  | F=10 | G=15 | H=1  |
| I=11 | J=5  | K=4  | L=14 |
| M=2  | N=16 | O=9  | P=7  |

Where The Red Fern Grows Vocabulary Word Search 1

Words are placed backwards, forward, diagonally, up and down. Clues listed below can help you find the words. Circle the hidden vocabulary words in the maze.

```
G N A W I N G C O M M O T I O N D V N N
N C Y W S Q U A B B L E X P H E E I O Q
I L D D O G N T S R V T Y X L N F C N W
X E O A V E U N T B A W L L D O I I C C
A A R Z P L Z E A R Y G U I E T A O H C
O V M E M D Z M C V S M S M T I N U A N
C E A D Y D L A L D L L N B A O T S L X
Z D N W R A I C E R O G G E O N P T A M
Z M T D O W N I D D U S K R L N C T N W
S P S Y T N G D G C G G E N G Y L X T J
C A Q O A G S E C N H U L E V E B Q L V
L C P U D X D R A D C L K L R L U P Y W
B E R S E R K P E C U L I A R I T Y V E
D D A Q R N T L K S E Y C D V W E W H L
D D N V P M C N U T O E A E D G T T E V
P O K E E N V H N L V B R B A Y I N G T
J M U X G S L A V E L E E O X L Z T N Z
N A J S R M M G I T D V S R J H L X U K
S I C Q E E G R U O C S S P L T V V L L
R N Y J V D G B E G R U D G I N G L Y B
```

Put out; extinguished (6)
A gentle touch or gesture of fondness, tenderness, or love (6)
A relatively calm interval (4)
Afflicting or worrying persistently (7)
An agitated disturbance (9)
Bending or flexing readily; pliable (6)
Boldly resisting (7)
Cause to be sorrowful; distress (6)
Crying or sobbing loudly; wailing (4)
Cunning (5)
Deep distress or misery, as from grief, wretchedness (3)
Deep ditch or channel cut in the earth by running water (5)
Depression or hollow, usually filled with deep mud or mire (6)
Destructively or frenetically violent (7)
Explored; investigated (6)
Expressed great, often malicious, pleasure or self-satisfaction (7)
Gently rubbing or pushing against (8)
Gone over extensively in the mind (6)
Having a fine, sharp cutting edge or point (4)
Latent but capable of being activated; sleeping (7)
Living by hunting (9)
Marked by an aggressive disposition; savage (7)
Marked by effortless grace (5)
Mental image; idea or conception (6)
Noisy quarrel, usually about a trivial matter (8)
Notable or distinctive feature or characteristic (11)
One that opposes, stands in the way of, or holds up progress (8)
Persuading or trying to persuade by pleading or flattery (7)
Pierced or penetrated (7)
Projecting overhang at the lower edge of a roof (5)
Protruding shelf over a fireplace (6)
Railroad or bus station (5)
Reluctantly (12)
Removed or forced out from a position or dwelling (9)
Satisfy (6)
Serious, grave, or solemn (5)
Shook with a slight, rapid, tremulous movement (8)
Strange and frightening (5)
Stunned (5)
Sudden forward movement or plunge (5)
Sudden sharp spasms of pain (5)
Territory over which rule or control is exercised (6)
The point beyond which an action is likely to begin (5)
The rate of speed at which something is done (4)
Unconcerned or indifferently (12)
Unpleasant or troublesome situation that is hard to get out of (11)
Uttering a deep, prolonged bark (6)
Walk with short steps that tilt the body from side to side (6)
Widespread, dreadful affliction and devastation (7)

Where The Red Fern Grows Vocabulary Word Search 1 Answer Key

Words are placed backwards, forward, diagonally, up and down. Clues listed below can help you find the words. Circle the hidden vocabulary words in the maze.

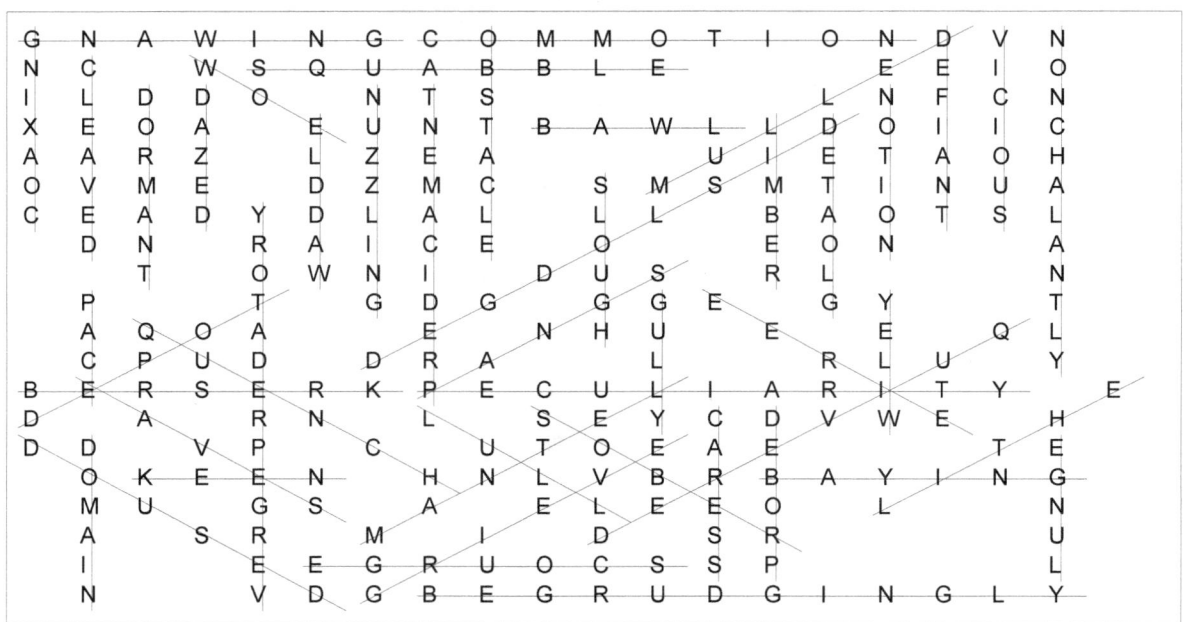

Put out; extinguished (6)
A gentle touch or gesture of fondness, tenderness, or love (6)
A relatively calm interval (4)
Afflicting or worrying persistently (7)
An agitated disturbance (9)
Bending or flexing readily; pliable (6)
Boldly resisting (7)
Cause to be sorrowful; distress (6)
Crying or sobbing loudly; wailing (4)
Cunning (5)
Deep distress or misery, as from grief, wretchedness (3)
Deep ditch or channel cut in the earth by running water (5)
Depression or hollow, usually filled with deep mud or mire (6)
Destructively or frenetically violent (7)
Explored; investigated (6)
Expressed great, often malicious, pleasure or self-satisfaction (7)
Gently rubbing or pushing against (8)
Gone over extensively in the mind (6)
Having a fine, sharp cutting edge or point (4)
Latent but capable of being activated; sleeping (7)
Living by hunting (9)
Marked by an aggressive disposition; savage (7)
Marked by effortless grace (5)
Mental image; idea or conception (6)
Noisy quarrel, usually about a trivial matter (8)

Notable or distinctive feature or characteristic (11)
One that opposes, stands in the way of, or holds up progress (8)
Persuading or trying to persuade by pleading or flattery (7)
Pierced or penetrated (7)
Projecting overhang at the lower edge of a roof (5)
Protruding shelf over a fireplace (6)
Railroad or bus station (5)
Reluctantly (12)
Removed or forced out from a position or dwelling (9)
Satisfy (6)
Serious, grave, or solemn (5)
Shook with a slight, rapid, tremulous movement (8)
Strange and frightening (5)
Stunned (5)
Sudden forward movement or plunge (5)
Sudden sharp spasms of pain (5)
Territory over which rule or control is exercised (6)
The point beyond which an action is likely to begin (5)
The rate of speed at which something is done (4)
Unconcerned or indifferently (12)
Unpleasant or troublesome situation that is hard to get out of (11)
Uttering a deep, prolonged bark (6)
Walk with short steps that tilt the body from side to side (6)
Widespread, dreadful affliction and devastation (7)

Where The Red Fern Grows Vocabulary Word Search 2

Words are placed backwards, forward, diagonally, up and down. Clues listed below can help you find the words. Circle the hidden vocabulary words in the maze.

```
M U L L E D G I N G E R L Y S Z N D G B
Z F D G N I X A O C G M Q P T L E Y N W
M A N T E L U L L Q R P Q Y B S O C I H
Z U Y H C N E U Q F U Y R R U Q G U L Z
L R T N A M R O D N O T I O N V S P G M
R I I N W J Q R R Q C N D T B Q N A N H
L D R C I B W U Q T S J H A G E X C A R
A S A K L C E C I T S A R D N C D E D D
S C I Z E E S R H V M T N E I A K Z D J
T O L F Y E A N S P E Y V R L R G W E Y
O M U N T W N V E E G R F P L E N W F T
N M C P O N M R E C R B E M A S V V I P
I O E J I T I X E D E K Q D U S E V A E
S T P A Z N C N R D V L M J Q J O N N S
H I M T G J M H I R W W D U S L G B T K
E O B S T A C L E T X A A V T S U R E F
D N G N I Y A B K D Z B D O Y Z L L W R
G R I E V E M F W E B S P D W S L M X H
B U S T L I N G D L Z E N Z L K Y Q Q B
W O E G L O A T E D D V K V C E M G Y G
```

Put out; extinguished (6)
A gentle touch or gesture of fondness, tenderness, or love (6)
A relatively calm interval (4)
An agitated disturbance (9)
Bending or flexing readily; pliable (6)
Boldly resisting (7)
Cause to be sorrowful; distress (6)
Crying or sobbing loudly; wailing (4)
Cunning (5)
Deep distress or misery, as from grief, wretchedness (3)
Deep ditch or channel cut in the earth by running water (5)
Depression or hollow, usually filled with deep mud or mire (6)
Destructively or frenetically violent (7)
Explored; investigated (6)
Expressed great, often malicious, pleasure or self-satisfaction (7)
Filled with sudden wonder or amazement (10)
Gone over extensively in the mind (6)
Hanging loosely or swinging (8)
Having a fine, sharp cutting edge or point (4)
Latent but capable of being activated; sleeping (7)
Living by hunting (9)
Made a V-shaped cut (7)
Marked by effortless grace (5)
Mental image; idea or conception (6)
Moving energetically and busily (8)

Noisy quarrel, usually about a trivial matter (8)
Notable or distinctive feature or characteristic (11)
One that opposes, stands in the way of, or holds up progress (8)
Persuading or trying to persuade by pleading or flattery (7)
Pierced or penetrated (7)
Preventing the free movement, action, or progress of (9)
Projecting overhang at the lower edge of a roof (5)
Protruding shelf over a fireplace (6)
Railroad or bus station (5)
Satisfy (6)
Screaming or crying loudly and harshly (9)
Serious, grave, or solemn (5)
Severe or radical in nature; extreme (7)
Shook with a slight, rapid, tremulous movement (8)
Strange and frightening (5)
Stunned (5)
Sudden forward movement or plunge (5)
Sudden sharp spasms of pain (5)
Territory over which rule or control is exercised (6)
The point beyond which an action is likely to begin (5)
The rate of speed at which something is done (4)
Uttering a deep, prolonged bark (6)
Walk with short steps that tilt the body from side to side (6)
Widespread, dreadful affliction and devastation (7)
With great care or delicacy; cautiously (8)

Where The Red Fern Grows Vocabulary Word Search 2 Answer Key

Words are placed backwards, forward, diagonally, up and down. Clues listed below can help you find the words. Circle the hidden vocabulary words in the maze.

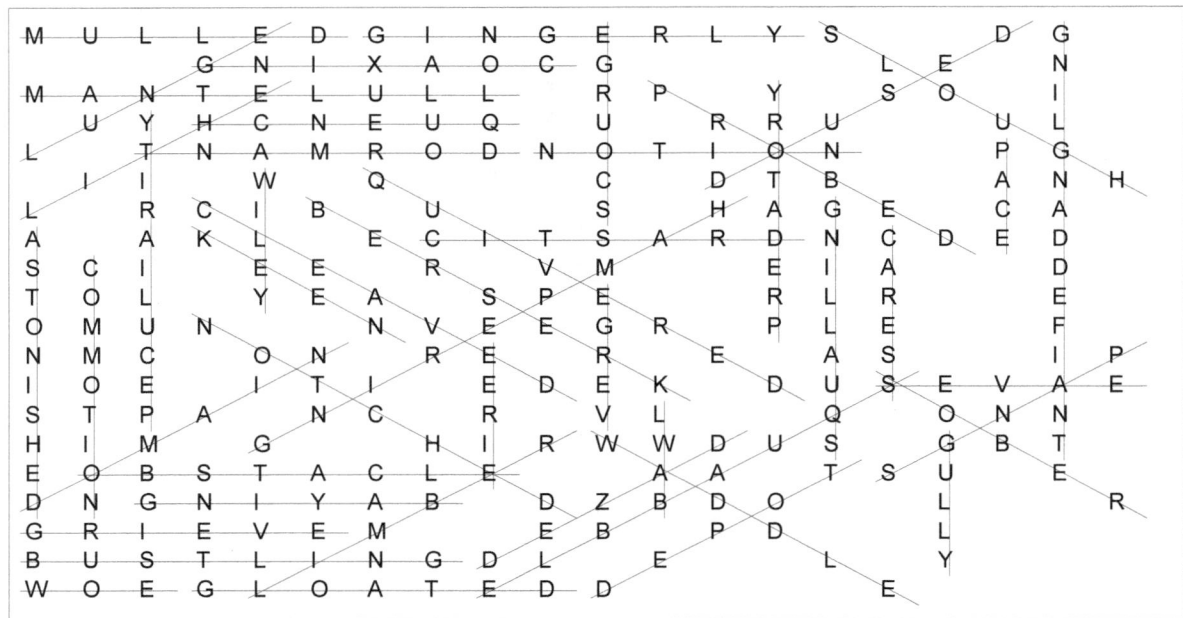

Put out; extinguished (6)
A gentle touch or gesture of fondness, tenderness, or love (6)
A relatively calm interval (4)
An agitated disturbance (9)
Bending or flexing readily; pliable (6)
Boldly resisting (7)
Cause to be sorrowful; distress (6)
Crying or sobbing loudly; wailing (4)
Cunning (5)
Deep distress or misery, as from grief, wretchedness (3)
Deep ditch or channel cut in the earth by running water (5)
Depression or hollow, usually filled with deep mud or mire (6)
Destructively or frenetically violent (7)
Explored; investigated (6)
Expressed great, often malicious, pleasure or self-satisfaction (7)
Filled with sudden wonder or amazement (10)
Gone over extensively in the mind (6)
Hanging loosely or swinging (8)
Having a fine, sharp cutting edge or point (4)
Latent but capable of being activated; sleeping (7)
Living by hunting (9)
Made a V-shaped cut (7)
Marked by effortless grace (5)
Mental image; idea or conception (6)
Moving energetically and busily (8)

Noisy quarrel, usually about a trivial matter (8)
Notable or distinctive feature or characteristic (11)
One that opposes, stands in the way of, or holds up progress (8)
Persuading or trying to persuade by pleading or flattery (7)
Pierced or penetrated (7)
Preventing the free movement, action, or progress of (9)
Projecting overhang at the lower edge of a roof (5)
Protruding shelf over a fireplace (6)
Railroad or bus station (5)
Satisfy (6)
Screaming or crying loudly and harshly (9)
Serious, grave, or solemn (5)
Severe or radical in nature; extreme (7)
Shook with a slight, rapid, tremulous movement (8)
Strange and frightening (5)
Stunned (5)
Sudden forward movement or plunge (5)
Sudden sharp spasms of pain (5)
Territory over which rule or control is exercised (6)
The point beyond which an action is likely to begin (5)
The rate of speed at which something is done (4)
Uttering a deep, prolonged bark (6)
Walk with short steps that tilt the body from side to side (6)
Widespread, dreadful affliction and devastation (7)
With great care or delicacy; cautiously (8)

Where The Red Fern Grows Vocabulary Word Search 3

Words are placed backwards, forward, diagonally, up and down. Words listed below are included in the maze. Circle the hidden vocabulary words in the maze.

```
B E G R U D G I N G L Y L R E G N I G N
B E Q D E M V E N E H I F I U P N N B R
M S R S Y N E I G L M R R L P O I W E K
Q A U S G K R K L B D E L M T Y C D L K
L O N W E E G T E B E Y N I A M O D L C
D U R T P R E R K A B Y O B T D A E I P
I B N M E T K Q W U O N B N D N X V G H
S S A G D L X V S Q R Y E U G C I A E D
L H N W E Q Y T I S P I G L S I N E R R
O K T N X S B K X C N V I L N T G L E X
D B B Z M S N J Q E I N L O O S L C N H
G G S L R E Y K V E G O T G D A B I T C
E V B T L R P N F A G C U N P R T L N S
D N C H A A O M D V H S O S V D W E K G
F Q U E N C H Q D E Z A D M U L L E D T
S H Z L D W L V D S F J Q Q M X S O M P
R C S Q L E B E M C B I P P T O R D F G
S L O U G H P A N G S T A W P M T Y N S
D G B U Q K Y O K B V C L N A G B I F M
L Z E L R E D G T T E H I N T D W A O D
B U R X L G R I E V E D T K G A D M W N
V R L I G C E P D Z K N H S N P H L F L
B B W L Q U I V E R E D E G W O E W E R
```

| AWL | DEFIANT | GULLY | PANGS |
| BAYING | DEPOT | HAMPERING | PROBED |
| BEGRUDGINGLY | DISLODGED | KEEN | QUENCH |
| BELLIGERENT | DOMAIN | LIMBER | QUIVERED |
| BERSERK | DORMANT | LITHE | SCOURGE |
| BUSTLING | DOUSED | LULL | SLOUGH |
| CARESS | DRASTIC | LUNGE | SOBER |
| CLEAVED | EAVES | MANTEL | SQUABBLE |
| COAXING | EERIE | MULLED | VERGE |
| COMMOTION | GINGERLY | NOTCHED | VICIOUS |
| CONVENIENT | GLOATED | NOTION | WADDLE |
| DANGLING | GNAWING | OBSTACLE | WILEY |
| DAZED | GRIEVE | PACE | WOE |

Where The Red Fern Grows Vocabulary Word Search 3 Answer Key

Words are placed backwards, forward, diagonally, up and down. Words listed below are included in the maze. Circle the hidden vocabulary words in the maze.

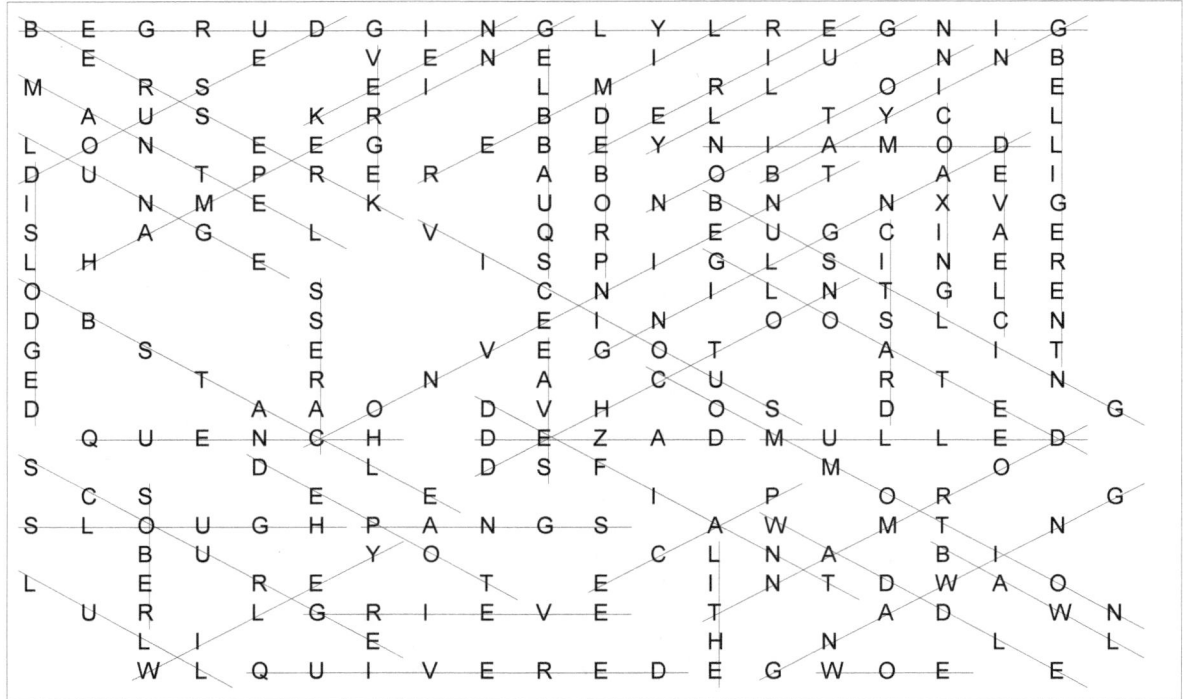

| BAWL | DEFIANT | GULLY | PANGS |
| --- | --- | --- | --- |
| BAYING | DEPOT | HAMPERING | PROBED |
| BEGRUDGINGLY | DISLODGED | KEEN | QUENCH |
| BELLIGERENT | DOMAIN | LIMBER | QUIVERED |
| BERSERK | DORMANT | LITHE | SCOURGE |
| BUSTLING | DOUSED | LULL | SLOUGH |
| CARESS | DRASTIC | LUNGE | SOBER |
| CLEAVED | EAVES | MANTEL | SQUABBLE |
| COAXING | EERIE | MULLED | VERGE |
| COMMOTION | GINGERLY | NOTCHED | VICIOUS |
| CONVENIENT | GLOATED | NOTION | WADDLE |
| DANGLING | GNAWING | OBSTACLE | WILEY |
| DAZED | GRIEVE | PACE | WOE |

Where The Red Fern Grows Vocabulary Word Search 4

Words are placed backwards, forward, diagonally, up and down. Words listed below are included in the maze. Circle the hidden vocabulary words in the maze.

```
D S R P N D Q S Y C Q T C S M P G S T X
N O T C H E D T E L U N G E B A Y I N G
L J Z L L F X O L E I A L P S N N G E N
B Y W D P I W U I A V M O D C G D T R L
X Z D R G A L M W V E R A E O S K E E N
L A R A G N S S C E R O T B U W C C G L
W P A B Z T L T Q D E D E O R P A Z I B
O R S A J E S V O U D N D R G P L E L D
B E T W E E D E D N A T O P E D H N L X
S D I L V R S R I U I B T T N T Y U E F
T I C A E I Q G S P M S B X I N S Z B M
A C E J I E L E L R D B H L K O P Z U Y
C A W W R R V D O E O P F E E Z N L S S
L M V H G L Q A D D M Y G O D T G I T W
E E P D N C H N G A A Y I B U Y X N L B
G N A W I N G G E T I S N E V N Y G I R
N T Q T R G U L D O N H G R I C D D N S
I T U L E H O I G R N D E S C A L E G J
X W E G P P L N U Y E D R E I R I S D R
A Q N H M J S G L L B Z L R O E M U H Z
O T C D A H B H L R T G Y K U S B O N Z
C Y H L H H B U Y J S Y Z M S S E D V T
S O B E R Z M S Q U A L L I N G R Y P N
```

| ASTONISHED | DOMAIN | LIMBER | PROBED |
| BAWL | DORMANT | LITHE | QUENCH |
| BAYING | DOUSED | LULL | QUIVERED |
| BELLIGERENT | DRASTIC | LUNGE | SCOURGE |
| BERSERK | DUMBFOUNDED | MANTEL | SLOUGH |
| BUSTLING | EAVES | MULLED | SOBER |
| CARESS | EERIE | NOTCHED | SQUABBLE |
| CLEAVED | GINGERLY | NOTION | SQUALLING |
| COAXING | GLOATED | NUZZLING | VERGE |
| DANGLING | GNAWING | OBSTACLE | VICIOUS |
| DAZED | GRIEVE | PACE | WADDLE |
| DEFIANT | GULLY | PANGS | WILEY |
| DEPOT | HAMPERING | PREDATORY | WOE |
| DISLODGED | KEEN | PREDICAMENT | |

Where The Red Fern Grows Vocabulary Word Search 4 Answer Key

Words are placed backwards, forward, diagonally, up and down. Words listed below are included in the maze. Circle the hidden vocabulary words in the maze.

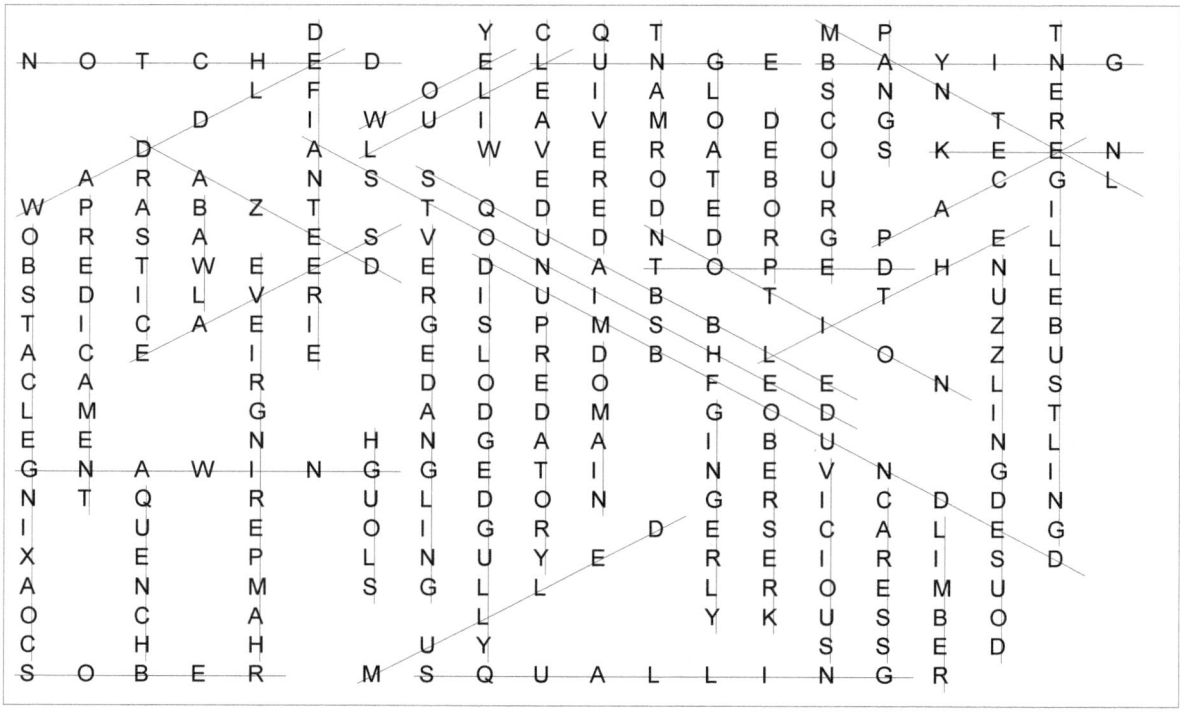

| ASTONISHED | DOMAIN | LIMBER | PROBED |
| BAWL | DORMANT | LITHE | QUENCH |
| BAYING | DOUSED | LULL | QUIVERED |
| BELLIGERENT | DRASTIC | LUNGE | SCOURGE |
| BERSERK | DUMBFOUNDED | MANTEL | SLOUGH |
| BUSTLING | EAVES | MULLED | SOBER |
| CARESS | EERIE | NOTCHED | SQUABBLE |
| CLEAVED | GINGERLY | NOTION | SQUALLING |
| COAXING | GLOATED | NUZZLING | VERGE |
| DANGLING | GNAWING | OBSTACLE | VICIOUS |
| DAZED | GRIEVE | PACE | WADDLE |
| DEFIANT | GULLY | PANGS | WILEY |
| DEPOT | HAMPERING | PREDATORY | WOE |
| DISLODGED | KEEN | PREDICAMENT | |

# Where The Red Fern Grows Vocabulary Crossword 1

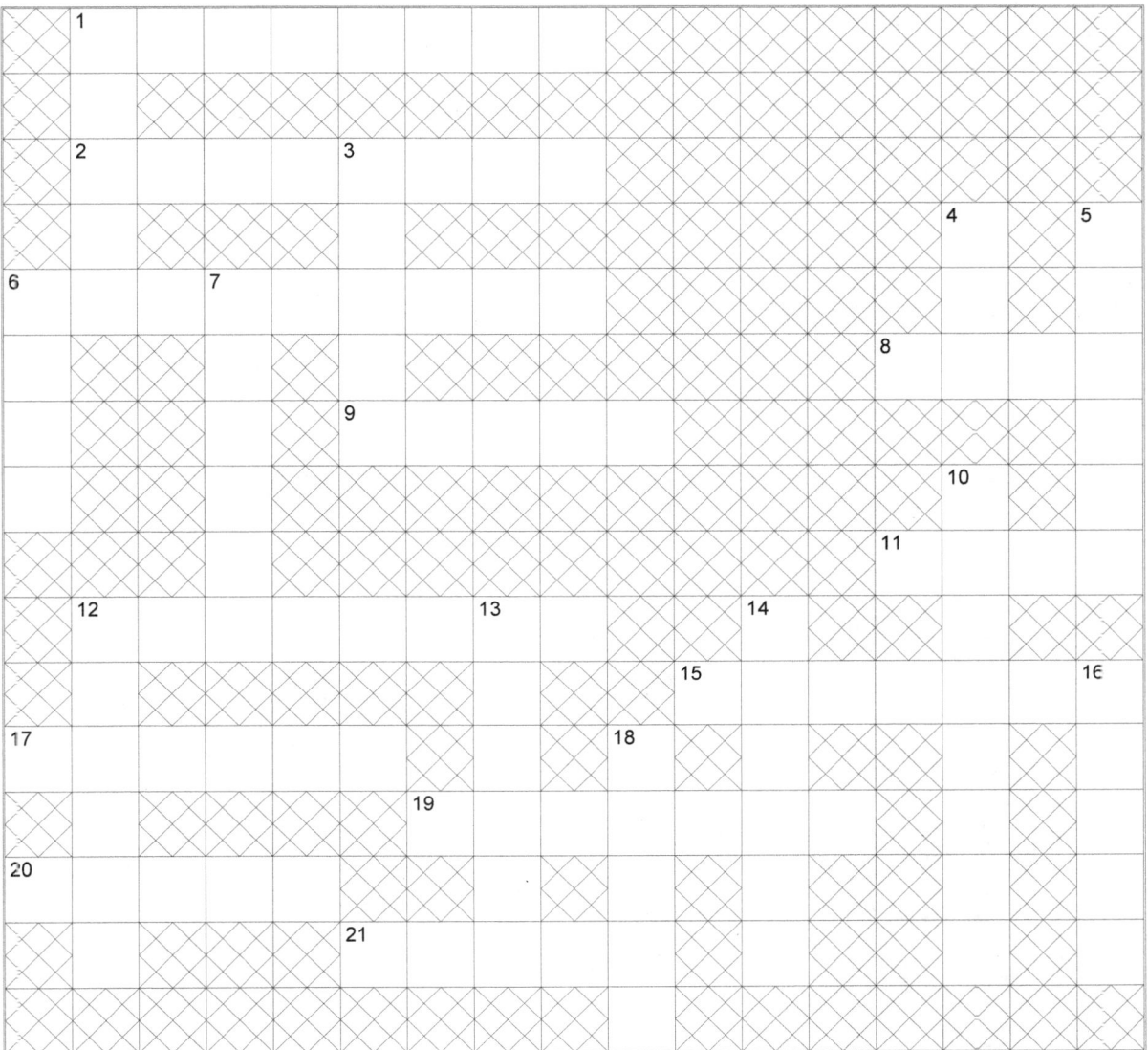

**Across**
1. Noisy quarrel, usually about a trivial matter
2. Moving energetically and busily
6. Living by hunting
8. Having a fine, sharp cutting edge or point
9. Projecting overhang at the lower edge of a roof
11. A relatively calm interval
12. Hanging loosely or swinging
15. Pierced or penetrated
17. Satisfy
19. Marked by an aggressive disposition; savage
20. The point beyond which an action is likely to begin
21. Sudden forward movement or plunge

**Down**
1. Serious, grave, or solemn
3. Marked by effortless grace
4. Deep distress or misery, as from grief, wretchedness
5. Protruding shelf over a fireplace
6. The rate of speed at which something is done
7. Territory over which rule or control is exercised
10. Shook with a slight, rapid, tremulous movement
12. Put out; extinguished
13. Mental image; idea or conception
14. Depression or hollow, usually filled with deep mud or mire
16. Stunned
18. Cunning

Where The Red Fern Grows Vocabulary Crossword 1 Answer Key

|   | 1 S | Q | U | A | B | B | L | E |   |   |   |   |   |   |
|---|---|---|---|---|---|---|---|---|---|---|---|---|---|---|
|   | O |   |   |   |   |   |   |   |   |   |   |   |   |   |
|   | 2 B | U | S | T | 3 L | I | N | G |   |   |   |   |   |   |
|   | E |   |   |   | I |   |   |   |   |   |   | 4 W |   | 5 M |
| 6 P | R | E | 7 D | A | T | O | R | Y |   |   |   | O |   | A |
| A |   |   | O |   | H |   |   |   |   |   | 8 K | E | E | N |
| C |   |   | M |   | 9 E | A | V | E | S |   |   |   |   | T |
| E |   |   | A |   |   |   |   |   |   |   | 10 Q |   |   | E |
|   |   |   | I |   |   |   |   |   |   | 11 L | U | L | L |   |
|   |   | 12 D | A | N | G | L | 13 I | N | G |   | 14 S |   | I |   |
|   |   | O |   |   |   |   | O |   | 15 C | L | E | A | V | 16 E |
| 17 Q | U | E | N | C | H |   | T |   | 18 W | O |   | E |   | A |
|   |   | S |   |   |   | 19 V | I | C | I | O | U | S |   | Z |
| 20 V | E | R | G | E |   |   | O |   | L |   | G |   | E | E |
|   |   | D |   |   | 21 L | U | N | G | E |   | H |   | D | D |
|   |   |   |   |   |   |   |   |   | Y |   |   |   |   |   |

Across
1. Noisy quarrel, usually about a trivial matter
2. Moving energetically and busily
6. Living by hunting
8. Having a fine, sharp cutting edge or point
9. Projecting overhang at the lower edge of a roof
11. A relatively calm interval
12. Hanging loosely or swinging
15. Pierced or penetrated
17. Satisfy
19. Marked by an aggressive disposition; savage
20. The point beyond which an action is likely to begin
21. Sudden forward movement or plunge

Down
1. Serious, grave, or solemn
3. Marked by effortless grace
4. Deep distress or misery, as from grief, wretchedness
5. Protruding shelf over a fireplace
6. The rate of speed at which something is done
7. Territory over which rule or control is exercised
10. Shook with a slight, rapid, tremulous movement
12. Put out; extinguished
13. Mental image; idea or conception
14. Depression or hollow, usually filled with deep mud or mire
16. Stunned
18. Cunning

# Where The Red Fern Grows Vocabulary Crossword 2

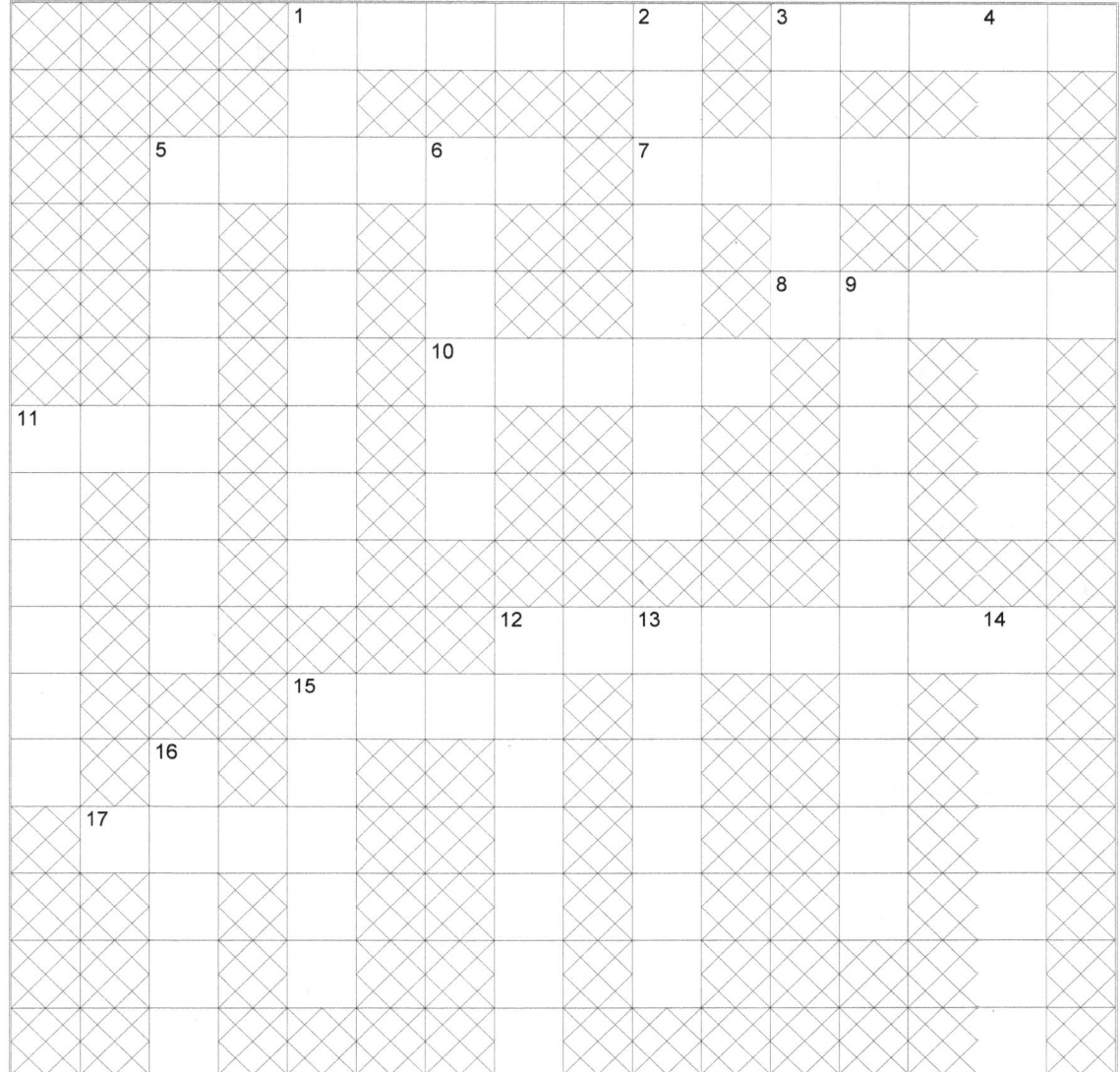

Across
1. Explored; investigated
3. Sudden forward movement or plunge
5. Satisfy
7. Mental image; idea or conception
8. Projecting overhang at the lower edge of a roof
10. Strange and frightening
11. Deep distress or misery, as from grief, wretchedness
12. Moving energetically and busily
15. The rate of speed at which something is done
17. Having a fine, sharp cutting edge or point

Down
1. Living by hunting
2. Hanging loosely or swinging
3. Marked by effortless grace
4. With great care or delicacy; cautiously
5. Shook with a slight, rapid, tremulous movement
6. A gentle touch or gesture of fondness, tenderness, or love
9. Filled with sudden wonder or amazement
11. Walk with short steps that tilt the body from side to side
12. Destructively or frenetically violent
13. Depression or hollow, usually filled with deep mud or mire
14. Afflicting or worrying persistently
15. Sudden sharp spasms of pain
16. The point beyond which an action is likely to begin

# Where The Red Fern Grows Vocabulary Crossword 2 Answer Key

|   |   |   | 1 P | R | O | B | E | 2 D |   | 3 L | U | N | 4 G | E |
|---|---|---|---|---|---|---|---|---|---|---|---|---|---|---|
|   |   |   | R |   |   |   |   | A |   | I |   |   | I |   |
|   |   | 5 Q | U | E | N | 6 C | H | 7 N | O | T | I | O | N |   |
|   |   |   | U |   |   | A |   | G |   | H |   |   | G |   |
|   |   |   | I |   |   | R |   | L |   | 8 E | 9 A | V | E | S |
|   |   |   | V |   |   | 10 E | R | I | E | S | R |   |   |   |
| 11 W | O | E |   | O |   | S |   | N |   | T | L |   |   |   |
| A |   | R |   | R |   | S |   | G |   | O | Y |   |   |   |
| D |   | E |   | Y |   |   |   |   |   | N |   |   |   |   |
| D |   | D |   |   |   | 12 B | U | 13 S | T | L | I | N | 14 G |   |
| L |   |   |   | 15 P | A | C | E |   | L |   |   | S | N |   |
| E |   | 16 V |   | A |   | E |   |   | O |   |   | H | A |   |
|   | 17 K | E | E | N |   | S |   |   | U |   |   | E | W |   |
|   |   | R |   | G |   | S |   |   | G |   |   | D | I |   |
|   |   | G |   | S |   | E |   |   | H |   |   |   | N |   |
|   |   | E |   |   |   | K |   |   |   |   |   |   | G |   |

Across
1. Explored; investigated
3. Sudden forward movement or plunge
5. Satisfy
7. Mental image; idea or conception
8. Projecting overhang at the lower edge of a roof
10. Strange and frightening
11. Deep distress or misery, as from grief, wretchedness
12. Moving energetically and busily
15. The rate of speed at which something is done
17. Having a fine, sharp cutting edge or point

Down
1. Living by hunting
2. Hanging loosely or swinging
3. Marked by effortless grace
4. With great care or delicacy; cautiously
5. Shook with a slight, rapid, tremulous movement
6. A gentle touch or gesture of fondness, tenderness, or love
9. Filled with sudden wonder or amazement
11. Walk with short steps that tilt the body from side to side
12. Destructively or frenetically violent
13. Depression or hollow, usually filled with deep mud or mire
14. Afflicting or worrying persistently
15. Sudden sharp spasms of pain
16. The point beyond which an action is likely to begin

# Where The Red Fern Grows Vocabulary Crossword 3

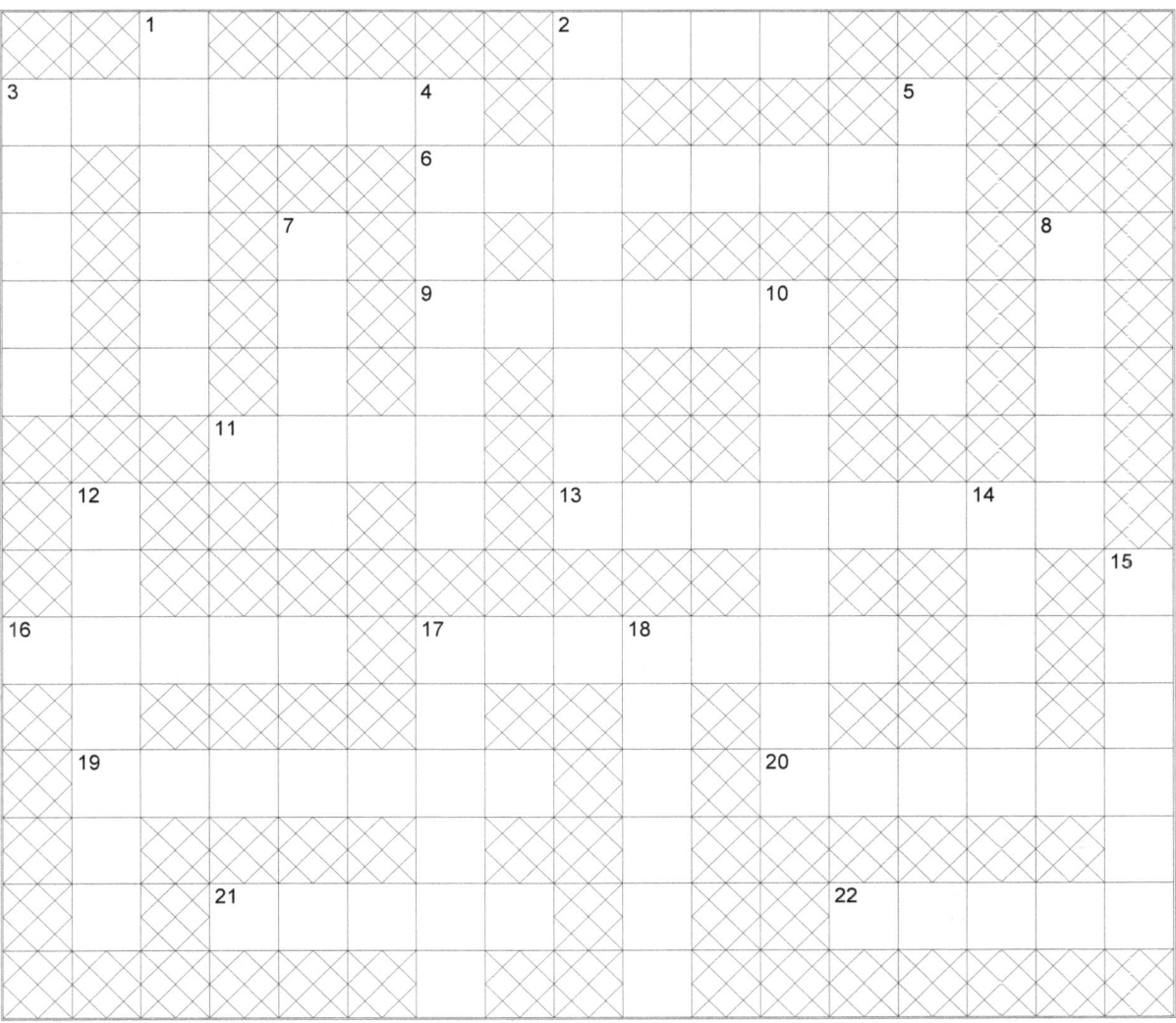

Across
2. Crying or sobbing loudly; wailing
3. Expressed great, often malicious, pleasure or self-satisfaction
6. One that opposes, stands in the way of, or holds up progress
9. Gone over extensively in the mind
11. Having a fine, sharp cutting edge or point
13. With great care or delicacy; cautiously
16. Strange and frightening
17. Severe or radical in nature; extreme
19. Marked by an aggressive disposition; savage
20. Cause to be sorrowful; distress
21. Stunned
22. Sudden sharp spasms of pain

Down
1. Mental image; idea or conception
2. Moving energetically and busily
3. Deep ditch or channel cut in the earth by running water
4. Latent but capable of being activated; sleeping
5. The point beyond which an action is likely to begin
7. Projecting overhang at the lower edge of a roof
8. Cunning
10. Hanging loosely or swinging
12. Pierced or penetrated
14. Sudden forward movement or plunge
15. A gentle touch or gesture of fondness, tenderness, or love
17. Put out; extinguished
18. Depression or hollow, usually filled with deep mud or mire

# Where The Red Fern Grows Vocabulary Crossword 3 Answer Key

|   | 1 N |   |   |   |   | 2 B | A | W | L |   |   |
|---|---|---|---|---|---|---|---|---|---|---|---|
| 3 G | L | O | A | T | E | D |   |   | 5 V |   |   |
| U |   |   |   | 6 O | B | S | T | A | C | L | E |
| L | 7 |   |   | R |   | T |   |   | R | 8 W |   |
| L | I | E |   | R |   |   |   | 10 D |   | I |   |
| L | O | A | 9 M | U | L | L | E | D |   | G |   |
| Y | N | V | A |   | I |   | A |   | E | I | L |
|   |   | 11 K | E | E | N |   | N |   |   | E |   |
|   | 12 C |   | S | T |   | 13 G | I | N | G | E | R | L | Y |
|   | L |   |   |   |   |   | L |   | 14 U | 15 C |
| 16 E | E | R | I | E |   | 17 D | R | A | 18 S | T | I | C | N | A |
|   | A |   |   |   |   | O |   |   | L |   | N | G | R |
| 19 V | I | C | I | O | U | S |   | 20 O | G | R | I | E | V | E |
|   | E |   |   |   |   | S |   | U |   |   |   | S |
|   | D |   | 21 D | A | Z | E | D | G |   | 22 P | A | N | G | S |
|   |   |   |   |   |   | D |   | H |   |   |   |

**Across**
2. Crying or sobbing loudly; wailing
3. Expressed great, often malicious, pleasure or self-satisfaction
6. One that opposes, stands in the way of, or holds up progress
9. Gone over extensively in the mind
11. Having a fine, sharp cutting edge or point
13. With great care or delicacy; cautiously
16. Strange and frightening
17. Severe or radical in nature; extreme
19. Marked by an aggressive disposition; savage
20. Cause to be sorrowful; distress
21. Stunned
22. Sudden sharp spasms of pain

**Down**
1. Mental image; idea or conception
2. Moving energetically and busily
3. Deep ditch or channel cut in the earth by running water
4. Latent but capable of being activated; sleeping
5. The point beyond which an action is likely to begin
7. Projecting overhang at the lower edge of a roof
8. Cunning
10. Hanging loosely or swinging
12. Pierced or penetrated
14. Sudden forward movement or plunge
15. A gentle touch or gesture of fondness, tenderness, or love
17. Put out; extinguished
18. Depression or hollow, usually filled with deep mud or mire

# Where The Red Fern Grows Vocabulary Crossword 4

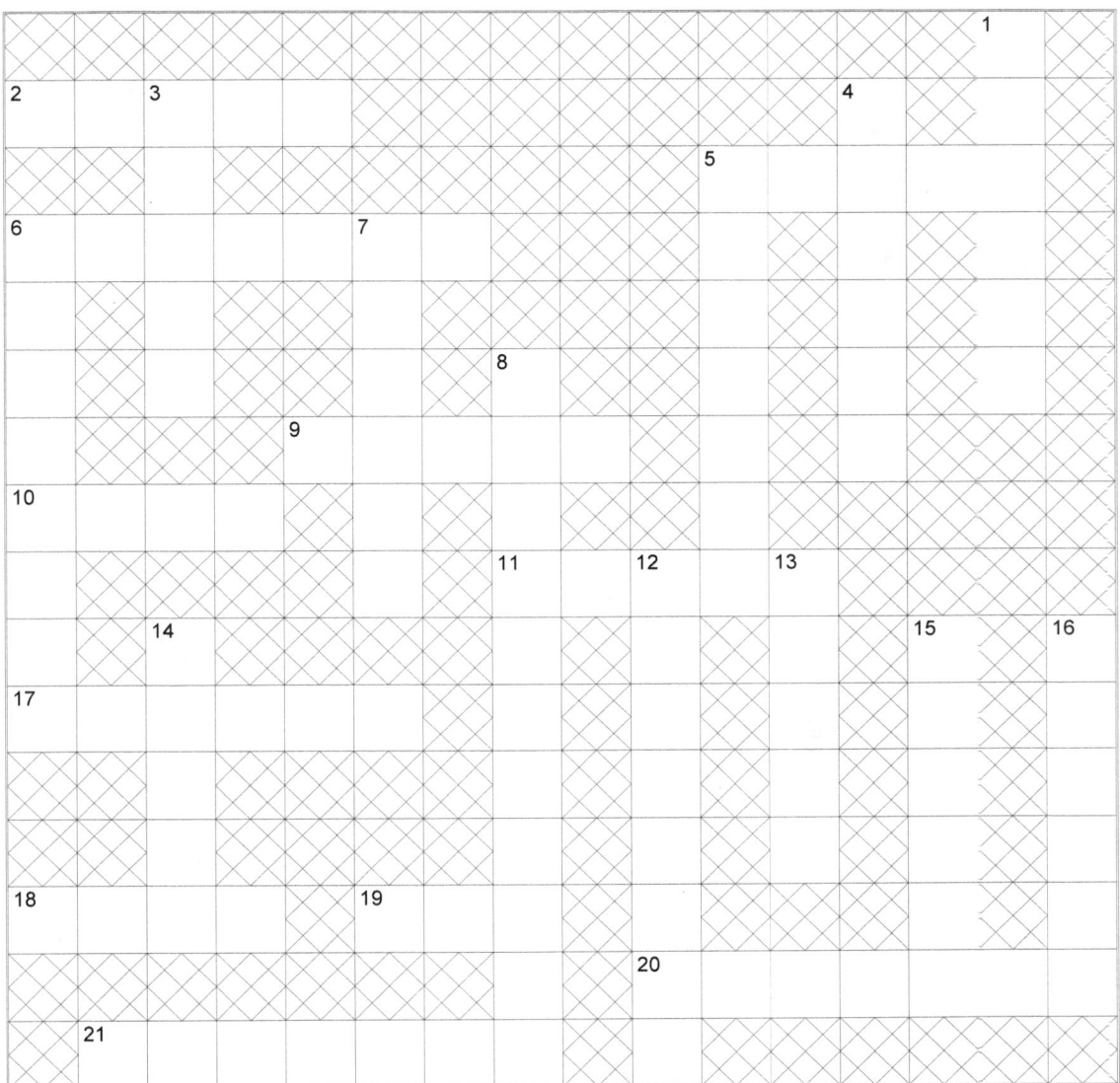

**Across**
2. Projecting overhang at the lower edge of a roof
5. Deep ditch or channel cut in the earth by running water
6. Latent but capable of being activated; sleeping
9. Cunning
10. A relatively calm interval
11. Sudden forward movement or plunge
17. Cause to be sorrowful; distress
18. Having a fine, sharp cutting edge or point
19. Deep distress or misery, as from grief, wretchedness
20. Made a V-shaped cut
21. Boldly resisting

**Down**
1. Uttering a deep, prolonged bark
3. The point beyond which an action is likely to begin
4. Depression or hollow, usually filled with deep mud or mire
5. Afflicting or worrying persistently
6. Hanging loosely or swinging
7. Mental image; idea or conception
8. Inclined to fight; hostile or aggressive
12. Gently rubbing or pushing against
13. Strange and frightening
14. Marked by effortless grace
15. Satisfy
16. Gone over extensively in the mind

# Where The Red Fern Grows Vocabulary Crossword 4 Answer Key

|   |   |   |   |   |   |   |   |   |   |   |   | 1 B |   |
|---|---|---|---|---|---|---|---|---|---|---|---|---|---|
| 2 E | A | 3 V | E | S |   |   |   |   |   | 4 S |   | A |   |
|   |   | E |   |   |   |   |   | 5 G | U | L | L | Y |   |
| 6 D | O | R | M | A | 7 N | T |   | N |   | O |   | I |   |
| A |   | G |   |   | O |   |   | A |   | U |   | N |   |
| N |   | E |   |   | T |   | 8 B | W |   | G |   | G |   |
| G |   |   |   | 9 W | I | L | E | Y |   | H |   |   |   |
| 10 L | U | L | L |   | O |   | L |   |   | I |   |   |   |
| I |   |   |   |   | N |   | 11 L | 12 U | 13 N | N | G | E |   |
| N |   | 14 L |   |   |   |   | I | U | E |   | 15 Q |   | 16 M |
| 17 G | R | I | E | V | E |   | G | Z | E |   | U |   | U |
|   |   | T |   |   |   |   | E | Z | R |   | E |   | L |
|   |   | H |   |   |   |   | R | L | I |   | N |   | L |
| 18 K | E | E | N |   | 19 W | O | E | I |   |   | C |   | E |
|   |   |   |   |   | N |   | 20 N | O | T | C | H | E | D |
|   |   | 21 D | E | F | I | A | N | T | G |   |   |   |   |

**Across**

2. Projecting overhang at the lower edge of a roof
5. Deep ditch or channel cut in the earth by running water
6. Latent but capable of being activated; sleeping
9. Cunning
10. A relatively calm interval
11. Sudden forward movement or plunge
17. Cause to be sorrowful; distress
18. Having a fine, sharp cutting edge or point
19. Deep distress or misery, as from grief, wretchedness
20. Made a V-shaped cut
21. Boldly resisting

**Down**

1. Uttering a deep, prolonged bark
3. The point beyond which an action is likely to begin
4. Depression or hollow, usually filled with deep mud or mire
5. Afflicting or worrying persistently
6. Hanging loosely or swinging
7. Mental image; idea or conception
8. Inclined to fight; hostile or aggressive
12. Gently rubbing or pushing against
13. Strange and frightening
14. Marked by effortless grace
15. Satisfy
16. Gone over extensively in the mind

Where The Red Fern Grows Vocabulary Juggle Letters 1

1. VSEAE = 1. _____
Projecting overhang at the lower edge of a roof

2. NLGLSQUAI = 2. _____
Screaming or crying loudly and harshly

3. ONONIT = 3. _____
Mental image; idea or conception

4. EGEEILRBLTN = 4. _____
Inclined to fight; hostile or aggressive

5. ALNEMT = 5. _____
Protruding shelf over a fireplace

6. ECTHODN = 6. _____
Made a V-shaped cut

7. YWELI = 7. _____
Cunning

8. UENQCH = 8. _____
Satisfy

9. HEIAOSNTSD = 9. _____
Filled with sudden wonder or amazement

10. NBIAGY = 10. _____
Uttering a deep, prolonged bark

11. GINWANG = 11. _____
Afflicting or worrying persistently

12. LEEAVDC = 12. _____
Pierced or penetrated

13. EADDZ = 13. _____
Stunned

14. ALTDOGE = 14. _____
Expressed great, often malicious, pleasure or self-satisfaction

15. TMIOMOCON = 15. _____
An agitated disturbance

Where The Red Fern Grows Vocabulary Juggle Letters 1 Answer Key

1. VSEAE = 1. EAVES
Projecting overhang at the lower edge of a roof

2. NLGLSQUAI = 2. SQUALLING
Screaming or crying loudly and harshly

3. ONONIT = 3. NOTION
Mental image; idea or conception

4. EGEEILRBLTN = 4. BELLIGERENT
Inclined to fight; hostile or aggressive

5. ALNEMT = 5. MANTEL
Protruding shelf over a fireplace

6. ECTHODN = 6. NOTCHED
Made a V-shaped cut

7. YWELI = 7. WILEY
Cunning

8. UENQCH = 8. QUENCH
Satisfy

9. HEIAOSNTSD = 9. ASTONISHED
Filled with sudden wonder or amazement

10. NBIAGY = 10. BAYING
Uttering a deep, prolonged bark

11. GINWANG = 11. GNAWING
Afflicting or worrying persistently

12. LEEAVDC = 12. CLEAVED
Pierced or penetrated

13. EADDZ = 13. DAZED
Stunned

14. ALTDOGE = 14. GLOATED
Expressed great, often malicious, pleasure or self-satisfaction

15. TMIOMOCON = 15. COMMOTION
An agitated disturbance

Where The Red Fern Grows Vocabulary Juggle Letters 2

1. HQNECU = 1. _____
Satisfy

2. LUYGL = 2. _____
Deep ditch or channel cut in the earth by running water

3. SPGNA = 3. _____
Sudden sharp spasms of pain

4. EBSOR = 4. _____
Serious, grave, or solemn

5. MOTNDAR = 5. _____
Latent but capable of being activated; sleeping

6. ENKE = 6. _____
Having a fine, sharp cutting edge or point

7. ENEGRETLIBL = 7. _____
Inclined to fight; hostile or aggressive

8. IGGEYLRN = 8. _____
With great care or delicacy; cautiously

9. REMILB = 9. _____
Bending or flexing readily; pliable

10. OUISICV =10. _____
Marked by an aggressive disposition; savage

11. NIBGGLRYUEGD =11. _____
Reluctantly

12. OEW =12. _____
Deep distress or misery, as from grief, wretchedness

13. ULNITSGB =13. _____
Moving energetically and busily

14. EVSAE =14. _____
Projecting overhang at the lower edge of a roof

15. IRPHENMAG =15. _____
Preventing the free movement, action, or progress of

Where The Red Fern Grows Vocabulary Juggle Letters 2 Answer Key

1. HQNECU = 1. QUENCH
Satisfy

2. LUYGL = 2. GULLY
Deep ditch or channel cut in the earth by running water

3. SPGNA = 3. PANGS
Sudden sharp spasms of pain

4. EBSOR = 4. SOBER
Serious, grave, or solemn

5. MOTNDAR = 5. DORMANT
Latent but capable of being activated; sleeping

6. ENKE = 6. KEEN
Having a fine, sharp cutting edge or point

7. ENEGRETLIBL = 7. BELLIGERENT
Inclined to fight; hostile or aggressive

8. IGGEYLRN = 8. GINGERLY
With great care or delicacy; cautiously

9. REMILB = 9. LIMBER
Bending or flexing readily; pliable

10. OUISICV = 10. VICIOUS
Marked by an aggressive disposition; savage

11. NIBGGLRYUEGD = 11. BEGRUDGINGLY
Reluctantly

12. OEW = 12. WOE
Deep distress or misery, as from grief, wretchedness

13. ULNITSGB = 13. BUSTLING
Moving energetically and busily

14. EVSAE = 14. EAVES
Projecting overhang at the lower edge of a roof

15. IRPHENMAG = 15. HAMPERING
Preventing the free movement, action, or progress of

Where The Red Fern Grows Vocabulary Juggle Letters 3

1. NWIAGNG = 1. _____
   Afflicting or worrying persistently

2. GREEV = 2. _____
   The point beyond which an action is likely to begin

3. LADNNGGI = 3. _____
   Hanging loosely or swinging

4. LWYEI = 4. _____
   Cunning

5. LBWA = 5. _____
   Crying or sobbing loudly; wailing

6. NOSHDISATE = 6. _____
   Filled with sudden wonder or amazement

7. DUNFUBDEMOD = 7. _____
   Filled with astonishment and perplexity

8. UELLMD = 8. _____
   Gone over extensively in the mind

9. OCIUISV = 9. _____
   Marked by an aggressive disposition; savage

10. ESCATBOL =10. _____
    One that opposes, stands in the way of, or holds up progress

11. INLNUZZG =11. _____
    Gently rubbing or pushing against

12. NAMTLE =12. _____
    Protruding shelf over a fireplace

13. EPDTO =13. _____
    Railroad or bus station

14. SUDOED =14. _____
    Put out; extinguished

15. SPAGN =15. _____
    Sudden sharp spasms of pain

Where The Red Fern Grows Vocabulary Juggle Letters 3 Answer Key

1. NWIAGNG = 1. GNAWING
   Afflicting or worrying persistently

2. GREEV = 2. VERGE
   The point beyond which an action is likely to begin

3. LADNNGGI = 3. DANGLING
   Hanging loosely or swinging

4. LWYEI = 4. WILEY
   Cunning

5. LBWA = 5. BAWL
   Crying or sobbing loudly; wailing

6. NOSHDISATE = 6. ASTONISHED
   Filled with sudden wonder or amazement

7. DUNFUBDEMOD = 7. DUMBFOUNDED
   Filled with astonishment and perplexity

8. UELLMD = 8. MULLED
   Gone over extensively in the mind

9. OCIUISV = 9. VICIOUS
   Marked by an aggressive disposition; savage

10. ESCATBOL = 10. OBSTACLE
    One that opposes, stands in the way of, or holds up progress

11. INLNUZZG = 11. NUZZLING
    Gently rubbing or pushing against

12. NAMTLE = 12. MANTEL
    Protruding shelf over a fireplace

13. EPDTO = 13. DEPOT
    Railroad or bus station

14. SUDOED = 14. DOUSED
    Put out; extinguished

15. SPAGN = 15. PANGS
    Sudden sharp spasms of pain

Where The Red Fern Grows Vocabulary Juggle Letters 4

1. LULL = 1. _____
A relatively calm interval

2. ETIREEGLNBL = 2. _____
Inclined to fight; hostile or aggressive

3. OUHLSG = 3. _____
Depression or hollow, usually filled with deep mud or mire

4. RYRPAEDTO = 4. _____
Living by hunting

5. GIWGNNA = 5. _____
Afflicting or worrying persistently

6. ADEZD = 6. _____
Stunned

7. TBLSAOEC = 7. _____
One that opposes, stands in the way of, or holds up progress

8. MBUFODEDNUD = 8. _____
Filled with astonishment and perplexity

9. AWLB = 9. _____
Crying or sobbing loudly; wailing

10. EEVRIG = 10. _____
Cause to be sorrowful; distress

11. INZLZUGN = 11. _____
Gently rubbing or pushing against

12. OELGTDA = 12. _____
Expressed great, often malicious, pleasure or self-satisfaction

13. RUEGOCS = 13. _____
Widespread, dreadful affliction and devastation

14. LGUYL = 14. _____
Deep ditch or channel cut in the earth by running water

15. SBULGNTI = 15. _____
Moving energetically and busily

Where The Red Fern Grows Vocabulary Juggle Letters 4 Answer Key

1. LULL = 1. LULL
   A relatively calm interval

2. ETIREEGLNBL = 2. BELLIGERENT
   Inclined to fight; hostile or aggressive

3. OUHLSG = 3. SLOUGH
   Depression or hollow, usually filled with deep mud or mire

4. RYRPAEDTO = 4. PREDATORY
   Living by hunting

5. GIWGNNA = 5. GNAWING
   Afflicting or worrying persistently

6. ADEZD = 6. DAZED
   Stunned

7. TBLSAOEC = 7. OBSTACLE
   One that opposes, stands in the way of, or holds up progress

8. MBUFODEDNUD = 8. DUMBFOUNDED
   Filled with astonishment and perplexity

9. AWLB = 9. BAWL
   Crying or sobbing loudly; wailing

10. EEVRIG = 10. GRIEVE
    Cause to be sorrowful; distress

11. INZLZUGN = 11. NUZZLING
    Gently rubbing or pushing against

12. OELGTDA = 12. GLOATED
    Expressed great, often malicious, pleasure or self-satisfaction

13. RUEGOCS = 13. SCOURGE
    Widespread, dreadful affliction and devastation

14. LGUYL = 14. GULLY
    Deep ditch or channel cut in the earth by running water

15. SBULGNTI = 15. BUSTLING
    Moving energetically and busily

| | |
|---|---|
| ASTONISHED | Filled with sudden wonder or amazement |
| BAWL | Crying or sobbing loudly; wailing |
| BAYING | Uttering a deep, prolonged bark |
| BEGRUDGINGLY | Reluctantly |
| BELLIGERENT | Inclined to fight; hostile or aggressive |
| BERSERK | Destructively or frenetically violent |

| | |
|---|---|
| BUSTLING | Moving energetically and busily |
| CARESS | A gentle touch or gesture of fondness, tenderness, or love |
| CLEAVED | Pierced or penetrated |
| COAXING | Persuading or trying to persuade by pleading or flattery |
| COMMOTION | An agitated disturbance |
| CONVENIENT | Easy to reach; accessible |

| | |
|---|---|
| DANGLING | Hanging loosely or swinging |
| DAZED | Stunned |
| DEFIANT | Boldly resisting |
| DEPOT | Railroad or bus station |
| DISLODGED | Removed or forced out from a position or dwelling |
| DOMAIN | Territory over which rule or control is exercised |

| | |
|---|---|
| DORMANT | Latent but capable of being activated; sleeping |
| DOUSED | Put out; extinguished |
| DRASTIC | Severe or radical in nature; extreme |
| DUMBFOUNDED | Filled with astonishment and perplexity |
| EAVES | Projecting overhang at the lower edge of a roof |
| EERIE | Strange and frightening |

| | |
|---|---|
| GINGERLY | With great care or delicacy; cautiously |
| GLOATED | Expressed great, often malicious, pleasure or self-satisfaction |
| GNAWING | Afflicting or worrying persistently |
| GRIEVE | Cause to be sorrowful; distress |
| GULLY | Deep ditch or channel cut in the earth by running water |
| HAMPERING | Preventing the free movement, action, or progress of |

| | |
|---|---|
| KEEN | Having a fine, sharp cutting edge or point |
| LIMBER | Bending or flexing readily; pliable |
| LITHE | Marked by effortless grace |
| LULL | A relatively calm interval |
| LUNGE | Sudden forward movement or plunge |
| MANTEL | Protruding shelf over a fireplace |

| | |
|---|---|
| MULLED | Gone over extensively in the mind |
| NONCHALANTLY | Unconcerned or indifferently |
| NOTCHED | Made a V-shaped cut |
| NOTION | Mental image; idea or conception |
| NUZZLING | Gently rubbing or pushing against |
| OBSTACLE | One that opposes, stands in the way of, or holds up progress |

| | |
|---|---|
| PACE | The rate of speed at which something is done |
| PANGS | Sudden sharp spasms of pain |
| PECULIARITY | Notable or distinctive feature or characteristic |
| PREDATORY | Living by hunting |
| PREDICAMENT | Unpleasant or troublesome situation that is hard to get out of |
| PROBED | Explored; investigated |

| | |
|---|---|
| QUENCH | Satisfy |
| QUIVERED | Shook with a slight, rapid, tremulous movement |
| SCOURGE | Widespread, dreadful affliction and devastation |
| SLOUGH | Depression or hollow, usually filled with deep mud or mire |
| SOBER | Serious, grave, or solemn |
| SQUABBLE | Noisy quarrel, usually about a trivial matter |

| | |
|---|---|
| SQUALLING | Screaming or crying loudly and harshly |
| VERGE | The point beyond which an action is likely to begin |
| VICIOUS | Marked by an aggressive disposition; savage |
| WADDLE | Walk with short steps that tilt the body from side to side |
| WILEY | Cunning |
| WOE | Deep distress or misery, as from grief, wretchedness |

## Where The Red Fern Grows Vocab

| MULLED | LIMBER | WOE | WILEY | QUIVERED |
|---|---|---|---|---|
| WADDLE | DOMAIN | PACE | DORMANT | NUZZLING |
| DANGLING | BELLIGERENT | FREE SPACE | ASTONISHED | BERSERK |
| BAWL | PROBED | PECULIARITY | DOUSED | CARESS |
| DISLODGED | NONCHALANTLY | PANGS | GNAWING | EAVES |

## Where The Red Fern Grows Vocab

| NOTCHED | NOTION | COAXING | MANTEL | GLOATED |
|---|---|---|---|---|
| DRASTIC | BAYING | DEPOT | SLOUGH | SQUABBLE |
| BEGRUDGINGLY | SCOURGE | FREE SPACE | VERGE | GINGERLY |
| LUNGE | PREDATORY | SOBER | OBSTACLE | GULLY |
| BUSTLING | DAZED | SQUALLING | LULL | COMMOTION |

Where The Red Fern Grows Vocab

| ASTONISHED | NOTCHED | CLEAVED | PREDICAMENT | LITHE |
|---|---|---|---|---|
| BAWL | DUMBFOUNDED | HAMPERING | DANGLING | DRASTIC |
| LULL | PREDATORY | FREE SPACE | PROBED | EERIE |
| NUZZLING | OBSTACLE | QUENCH | NONCHALANTLY | VERGE |
| CARESS | DAZED | LIMBER | COAXING | KEEN |

Where The Red Fern Grows Vocab

| BUSTLING | PECULIARITY | BEGRUDGINGLY | LUNGE | SOBER |
|---|---|---|---|---|
| WADDLE | DEFIANT | GULLY | PACE | SQUABBLE |
| GINGERLY | DOMAIN | FREE SPACE | GLOATED | SLOUGH |
| COMMOTION | GNAWING | DEPOT | NOTION | DOUSED |
| BELLIGERENT | QUIVERED | BAYING | MANTEL | BERSERK |

## Where The Red Fern Grows Vocab

| NOTION | BERSERK | DEPOT | LULL | DEFIANT |
|---|---|---|---|---|
| SQUALLING | LITHE | DOUSED | PANGS | DANGLING |
| SQUABBLE | BAWL | FREE SPACE | GINGERLY | OBSTACLE |
| BEGRUDGINGLY | QUENCH | COMMOTION | VICIOUS | GRIEVE |
| LIMBER | BELLIGERENT | PACE | SOBER | MULLED |

## Where The Red Fern Grows Vocab

| GLOATED | CONVENIENT | EERIE | PREDICAMENT | NUZZLING |
|---|---|---|---|---|
| EAVES | QUIVERED | WILEY | DAZED | DOMAIN |
| DISLODGED | WOE | FREE SPACE | HAMPERING | CARESS |
| SLOUGH | NONCHALANTLY | NOTCHED | MANTEL | BUSTLING |
| PECULIARITY | KEEN | COAXING | ASTONISHED | PROBED |

Where The Red Fern Grows Vocab

| QUENCH | PACE | WADDLE | SOBER | MANTEL |
|---|---|---|---|---|
| BAWL | GINGERLY | EAVES | PECULIARITY | DRASTIC |
| NOTION | PREDICAMENT | FREE SPACE | BELLIGERENT | BAYING |
| DEPOT | COMMOTION | SQUABBLE | DOMAIN | GNAWING |
| GLOATED | PANGS | SQUALLING | WILEY | KEEN |

Where The Red Fern Grows Vocab

| GRIEVE | DAZED | QUIVERED | ASTONISHED | LUNGE |
|---|---|---|---|---|
| CLEAVED | LITHE | COAXING | DANGLING | EERIE |
| NOTCHED | SLOUGH | FREE SPACE | CARESS | CONVENIENT |
| MULLED | OBSTACLE | NUZZLING | LIMBER | BERSERK |
| DOUSED | WOE | LULL | HAMPERING | SCOURGE |

## Where The Red Fern Grows Vocab

| DEFIANT | BELLIGERENT | GNAWING | LIMBER | PANGS |
|---|---|---|---|---|
| COAXING | VICIOUS | WADDLE | GINGERLY | OBSTACLE |
| NONCHALANTLY | SQUABBLE | FREE SPACE | CONVENIENT | DEPOT |
| PREDATORY | QUIVERED | DOMAIN | CLEAVED | GULLY |
| WILEY | GRIEVE | DAZED | LUNGE | BAYING |

## Where The Red Fern Grows Vocab

| DORMANT | EERIE | CARESS | BAWL | BERSERK |
|---|---|---|---|---|
| BEGRUDGINGLY | KEEN | NOTION | PACE | NOTCHED |
| NUZZLING | DRASTIC | FREE SPACE | DISLODGED | SLOUGH |
| PECULIARITY | SOBER | MULLED | WOE | DUMBFOUNDED |
| MANTEL | BUSTLING | PREDICAMENT | DOUSED | COMMOTION |

## Where The Red Fern Grows Vocab

| | | | | |
|---|---|---|---|---|
| BUSTLING | BERSERK | DANGLING | VERGE | WILEY |
| GRIEVE | SLOUGH | PECULIARITY | CARESS | PREDICAMENT |
| GLOATED | BELLIGERENT | FREE SPACE | MANTEL | DEPOT |
| OBSTACLE | PACE | SCOURGE | LULL | GULLY |
| DAZED | BAWL | DOUSED | SQUABBLE | BEGRUDGINGLY |

## Where The Red Fern Grows Vocab

| | | | | |
|---|---|---|---|---|
| LUNGE | NUZZLING | NOTION | PROBED | MULLED |
| CLEAVED | PANGS | NONCHALANTLY | DOMAIN | COAXING |
| DRASTIC | ASTONISHED | FREE SPACE | DEFIANT | QUIVERED |
| CONVENIENT | DUMBFOUNDED | HAMPERING | WADDLE | COMMOTION |
| LIMBER | DORMANT | QUENCH | GINGERLY | GNAWING |

## Where The Red Fern Grows Vocab

| SQUABBLE | BERSERK | BAYING | GULLY | NOTION |
|---|---|---|---|---|
| PECULIARITY | LULL | DUMBFOUNDED | GINGERLY | LUNGE |
| DORMANT | DOMAIN | FREE SPACE | DRASTIC | GNAWING |
| PREDATORY | PANGS | LIMBER | NONCHALANTLY | NUZZLING |
| SOBER | BAWL | ASTONISHED | PREDICAMENT | VICIOUS |

## Where The Red Fern Grows Vocab

| PACE | NOTCHED | MULLED | PROBED | KEEN |
|---|---|---|---|---|
| DEFIANT | SCOURGE | OBSTACLE | DISLODGED | WILEY |
| GLOATED | DANGLING | FREE SPACE | BELLIGERENT | WADDLE |
| DAZED | EAVES | DOUSED | QUIVERED | CONVENIENT |
| EERIE | HAMPERING | COMMOTION | DEPOT | QUENCH |

Where The Red Fern Grows Vocab

| GINGERLY | LIMBER | NUZZLING | WILEY | SCOURGE |
|---|---|---|---|---|
| EAVES | BELLIGERENT | PANGS | CONVENIENT | KEEN |
| DEPOT | DEFIANT | FREE SPACE | VICIOUS | PROBED |
| WOE | NOTION | GULLY | VERGE | SOBER |
| DRASTIC | PREDATORY | LITHE | WADDLE | MULLED |

Where The Red Fern Grows Vocab

| CARESS | GNAWING | DORMANT | DOUSED | DUMBFOUNDED |
|---|---|---|---|---|
| EERIE | LULL | PACE | QUENCH | PECULIARITY |
| SQUABBLE | DOMAIN | FREE SPACE | QUIVERED | BUSTLING |
| GLOATED | ASTONISHED | MANTEL | BAYING | OBSTACLE |
| CLEAVED | BERSERK | BEGRUDGINGLY | GRIEVE | NONCHALANTLY |

## Where The Red Fern Grows Vocab

| VERGE | SOBER | EERIE | DISLODGED | SCOURGE |
|---|---|---|---|---|
| NUZZLING | GRIEVE | MULLED | WADDLE | LITHE |
| HAMPERING | GULLY | FREE SPACE | DUMBFOUNDED | LUNGE |
| OBSTACLE | PREDICAMENT | DRASTIC | QUENCH | COAXING |
| PREDATORY | BAWL | DOMAIN | WILEY | KEEN |

## Where The Red Fern Grows Vocab

| GNAWING | BERSERK | COMMOTION | NOTCHED | PROBED |
|---|---|---|---|---|
| BUSTLING | LULL | PACE | VICIOUS | DEFIANT |
| CONVENIENT | DORMANT | FREE SPACE | SQUALLING | MANTEL |
| CARESS | NOTION | PANGS | DEPOT | QUIVERED |
| GLOATED | LIMBER | BEGRUDGINGLY | WOE | SLOUGH |

## Where The Red Fern Grows Vocab

| | | | | |
|---|---|---|---|---|
| SQUALLING | PANGS | DAZED | NONCHALANTLY | DANGLING |
| COMMOTION | COAXING | WILEY | PREDICAMENT | CONVENIENT |
| NOTION | MULLED | FREE SPACE | EAVES | LIMBER |
| LUNGE | DEFIANT | GULLY | CARESS | ASTONISHED |
| QUIVERED | DEPOT | PREDATORY | NUZZLING | DISLODGED |

## Where The Red Fern Grows Vocab

| | | | | |
|---|---|---|---|---|
| SLOUGH | VERGE | BUSTLING | SQUABBLE | LITHE |
| BERSERK | DRASTIC | DORMANT | BELLIGERENT | GRIEVE |
| VICIOUS | HAMPERING | FREE SPACE | KEEN | OBSTACLE |
| DUMBFOUNDED | BEGRUDGINGLY | SOBER | QUENCH | PECULIARITY |
| BAWL | GLOATED | DOUSED | DOMAIN | LULL |

Where The Red Fern Grows Vocab

| PREDICAMENT | WILEY | NOTION | BEGRUDGINGLY | WOE |
| --- | --- | --- | --- | --- |
| EAVES | SLOUGH | DEPOT | BUSTLING | PANGS |
| DANGLING | LULL | FREE SPACE | SOBER | GLOATED |
| CONVENIENT | BELLIGERENT | DUMBFOUNDED | QUIVERED | ASTONISHED |
| LIMBER | CLEAVED | GULLY | DISLODGED | SQUABBLE |

Where The Red Fern Grows Vocab

| COMMOTION | NONCHALANTLY | DEFIANT | PECULIARITY | PROBED |
| --- | --- | --- | --- | --- |
| HAMPERING | CARESS | PREDATORY | NOTCHED | NUZZLING |
| GRIEVE | SQUALLING | FREE SPACE | GNAWING | PACE |
| SCOURGE | GINGERLY | COAXING | KEEN | DAZED |
| VICIOUS | QUENCH | BERSERK | MULLED | DORMANT |

### Where The Red Fern Grows Vocab

| | | | | |
|---|---|---|---|---|
| CARESS | GLOATED | LITHE | SLOUGH | DOUSED |
| GULLY | LULL | GNAWING | SCOURGE | NONCHALANTLY |
| DAZED | SQUABBLE | FREE SPACE | PANGS | HAMPERING |
| CLEAVED | PROBED | BELLIGERENT | BAWL | DRASTIC |
| DUMBFOUNDED | VERGE | LUNGE | QUIVERED | PREDATORY |

### Where The Red Fern Grows Vocab

| | | | | |
|---|---|---|---|---|
| SQUALLING | WOE | MANTEL | PREDICAMENT | DORMANT |
| LIMBER | NOTION | EAVES | CONVENIENT | BUSTLING |
| DEPOT | OBSTACLE | FREE SPACE | QUENCH | BAYING |
| DEFIANT | NUZZLING | MULLED | COMMOTION | WADDLE |
| DOMAIN | BEGRUDGINGLY | BERSERK | VICIOUS | EERIE |

Where The Red Fern Grows Vocab

| EERIE | BUSTLING | GLOATED | CARESS | VICIOUS |
|---|---|---|---|---|
| DAZED | SLOUGH | PANGS | MANTEL | DOUSED |
| ASTONISHED | PREDICAMENT | FREE SPACE | DORMANT | DEFIANT |
| DISLODGED | GULLY | NUZZLING | WADDLE | LULL |
| CLEAVED | KEEN | DOMAIN | WILEY | SQUABBLE |

Where The Red Fern Grows Vocab

| SOBER | GNAWING | BERSERK | COMMOTION | HAMPERING |
|---|---|---|---|---|
| WOE | CONVENIENT | DUMBFOUNDED | BELLIGERENT | NONCHALANTLY |
| PACE | LIMBER | FREE SPACE | NOTCHED | LITHE |
| PREDATORY | QUIVERED | LUNGE | COAXING | QUENCH |
| PROBED | BAWL | GRIEVE | DRASTIC | VERGE |

Where The Red Fern Grows Vocab

| CLEAVED | DORMANT | QUENCH | VICIOUS | GRIEVE |
|---|---|---|---|---|
| CONVENIENT | PREDATORY | VERGE | OBSTACLE | DOMAIN |
| LULL | DANGLING | FREE SPACE | DEFIANT | SQUALLING |
| EERIE | MANTEL | GINGERLY | BEGRUDGINGLY | DISLODGED |
| CARESS | ASTONISHED | PROBED | DOUSED | WILEY |

Where The Red Fern Grows Vocab

| SOBER | DAZED | HAMPERING | NUZZLING | BUSTLING |
|---|---|---|---|---|
| GNAWING | DRASTIC | DEPOT | MULLED | PECULIARITY |
| BERSERK | BELLIGERENT | FREE SPACE | WADDLE | PANGS |
| SQUABBLE | COMMOTION | SCOURGE | QUIVERED | NOTCHED |
| PREDICAMENT | LUNGE | SLOUGH | GULLY | PACE |

Where The Red Fern Grows Vocab

| LUNGE | GINGERLY | NOTION | DORMANT | ASTONISHED |
|---|---|---|---|---|
| DEPOT | GRIEVE | SLOUGH | NONCHALANTLY | NUZZLING |
| VERGE | OBSTACLE | FREE SPACE | LIMBER | GLOATED |
| QUIVERED | COAXING | DISLODGED | BELLIGERENT | CLEAVED |
| BAWL | LITHE | VICIOUS | KEEN | WADDLE |

Where The Red Fern Grows Vocab

| GULLY | DRASTIC | CARESS | DAZED | PREDICAMENT |
|---|---|---|---|---|
| BUSTLING | MULLED | EAVES | EERIE | BERSERK |
| LULL | DUMBFOUNDED | FREE SPACE | WOE | SQUABBLE |
| SQUALLING | MANTEL | PECULIARITY | PANGS | DEFIANT |
| CONVENIENT | BEGRUDGINGLY | WILEY | COMMOTION | PACE |

Where The Red Fern Grows Vocab

| LULL | NOTCHED | QUENCH | PREDICAMENT | SCOURGE |
|---|---|---|---|---|
| EAVES | SOBER | VERGE | GNAWING | CONVENIENT |
| BELLIGERENT | VICIOUS | FREE SPACE | SQUABBLE | CLEAVED |
| DEPOT | GRIEVE | DAZED | ASTONISHED | LIMBER |
| LUNGE | MULLED | SQUALLING | GLOATED | MANTEL |

Where The Red Fern Grows Vocab

| PACE | LITHE | NONCHALANTLY | DUMBFOUNDED | OBSTACLE |
|---|---|---|---|---|
| PECULIARITY | BERSERK | PREDATORY | KEEN | HAMPERING |
| QUIVERED | PANGS | FREE SPACE | WOE | DANGLING |
| DOMAIN | EERIE | GULLY | NOTION | DISLODGED |
| BUSTLING | BEGRUDGINGLY | GINGERLY | NUZZLING | CARESS |

www.ingramcontent.com/pod-product-compliance
Lightning Source LLC
LaVergne TN
LVHW081538060526
838200LV00048B/2121